Access
to
Qur'anic Arabic

TEXTBOOK

Access to to Qur'anic Arabic

TEXTBOOK

AbdulWahid Hamid

 MELS

◆

In the name of God, most Gracious, most Merciful

O you who have believed!
Respond to (the call of) God and to the Messenger
when he calls you
to what gives you life.
(Surah al-Anfal, 8: 24)

Published by MELS
61 Alexandra Road, Hendon
London NW4 2RX, UK
Tel: 0181 202 1799
Fax: 0181 201 5924
email: ahamid@webstar.co.uk

© MELS 1998

ISBN 0 948196 15 7 - Textbook

ISBN 0 948196 16 5 - Workbook

ISBN 0 948196 17 3 - Selections

Design by Zafar Malik
Arabic typesetting and layout by Abdulkader Khattab,
Compumedia Ltd, London
English text set in Frutiger Roman and Arabic text
set in Obeid using An-Nashir as-Sahafi™ software
Cover illustration: Detail, Bait ul Qur'an, Lahore by Shakir Ali
Printed and bound by The Cromwell Press,
Trowbridge, Wiltshire, UK.

Contents

Contents

Introduction

Most people need to know Arabic primarily to understand the Qur'an. This **Access to Qur'anic Arabic** course is an attempt to meet part of this need.

Aim

The aim is to get users to understand much of what they read as quickly and effortlessly as possible. The course seeks to do this by providing a graded introduction to the grammar and structure of Qur'anic Arabic and using words which occur very frequently in the Qur'an.

This course does not teach people to speak Arabic or to translate into Arabic.

Requirements

We assume that users can read and write the Arabic script. Those who cannot do so are referred to the MELS Easy Steps in Arabic materials for reading and writing the Arabic script and reading the Qur'an. A good grasp of English will be useful.

Course Materials

1. The **Textbook** covers the basic grammar and structure of Arabic using Qur'anic words, phrases and sentences almost entirely. (The few non-Qur'anic phrases and sentences used are pointed out.) The page layout and design of the Units in the textbook should make it easy to follow.

Initially, only a limited vocabulary is used based on its frequency of occurrence in the Qur'an. The Textbook contains three Word Lists. The first has words which, with their derivatives, occur over 100 times in the Qur'an. Word List 2 has such words occurring between 50 and 100 times. Word List 3 has such words occurring between 25 and 49 times. (Not all derivatives are listed.)

This approach has two benefits. Students will not be burdened with a very large vocabulary from the outset. By mastering the select vocabulary, they will be able to understand much and quickly.

2. Two audiocassette tapes contain a recording of the Qur'anic text and English translation for each unit of the Texbook.

3. A separate **Workbook** has exercises for each Unit of the Textbook and gives much-needed further practice in the grammar and structure of the language. Phrases and sentences used in the Workbook are also from the Qur'an and the vocabulary is mainly that which is used in the textbook.

4. An important part of this course is the book **Selections from the Qur'an** which has passages that feature the select vocabulary and illustrate points of grammar and structure covered in the Texbook. The Selections are presented with parallel translations into English and notes on language and structure. The meaning of words not included in the three word lists is given. The three Wordlists are combined into one in the book of Selections.

5. Three audiocassette tapes contain the full recording of the Selections from the Qur'an.

Self-study

This course has been designed for self-study as well as for use in classroom situations. Even if used as a self-study course, the guidance of a competent teacher may at times be necessary.

Further Study

We hope this course will stimulate users to go further to a more detailed study of the Qur'an and of Arabic. For those who want to go further, we hope this book will be a useful starting point. It should of course be pointed out that the grammar and structure of Qur'anic Arabic and classical and modern literary Arabic is substantially the same, thanks largely to the enduring importance and preservation of the Qur'an itself. Some suggestions for further study are included at the end of this Textbook.

Testing

This course has been developed with and tested on children and adults, including family and friends. We are grateful to all those who took part in the process and pray that they and others who use it will go on to gain a better understanding of the Qur'an, the better to appreciate it, follow it, and be inspired by it throughout their lives.

Comments & suggestions

We will be most grateful for any comments and suggestions for improvement from users of this course, including teachers, students and those engaged in self-study.

Introduction

Acknowledgements

Alhamdu lillah - all praise and thanks is due to God, the Sustainer of all creation. May He bless all who have taught and advised, supported and encouraged me in this work over the years - especially my dear parents whose knowledge of Arabic was little but whose love for Islam was firm. Of so many others, I hope I will be forgiven for mentioning only a few here. Among them is AbdulQayyum Khan of Guyana (now in Toronto) who came to Trinidad and taught me, at the age of eighteen, to read and write the Arabic script; Ebrahimsa Mohammed for his guidance and friendship over a generation; M Hashir Faruqi for his wise counsel; Jamil Sherif and Muhammad Yasien Khan of New Jersey for lessons in dedication and constancy; Iqbal Sacranie for his keen interest in this work and Zafar Malik for his time and his precious skills - not limited to graphics.

I am grateful to Mr Salim Kayani, a devoted and profound Qur'anic scholar, Hashim Abdur Rahman, a graduate of the University of Madinah and Esam Mustafa of the Palestinian charity Interpal for going through the manuscripts and for their many helpful comments. I am particularly indebted to Dr Muhammad Farid Elshayyal, Senior Lecturer in the Department of Arabic at the University of Westminster, for his close scrutiny of the texts and for his corrections and detailed suggestions.

I would like to thank Raashid Ayyub for introducing me to AbdulKadir Khattab without whose help these books would not have reached their present form. Brother AbdulKadir not only has a superb range of computer skills but his unfailing trust and cheerfulness made working on this project such a great pleasure. I thank his wife Namat for her hospitality and for putting up with long and often odd hours of work.

I am also grateful to my nephew Asad Hamid and my daughter Zahra for their efficient computing skills; my daughter Kaamileh for her critical eye and graphic solutions; and my wife Azieza for her constant encouragement and invaluable advice as an experienced teacher. And to Mike Arkell and his colleagues at Cromwell Press, I must say how greatly I appreciate and value their professionalism and courtesy.

We pray that Allah Almighty will accept our efforts and that this attempt will be helpful in taking us along the way of discovering the Qur'an - the human being's only authentic link with Reality - and patterning our lives by it. And when the Hour comes, may the Qur'an be a testimony for us, and not against us.

We seek His help and guidance and we turn to Him in repentance and gratitude. And may His peace and blessings be on His noble messenger, the unlettered Prophet, the shining beacon.

AbdulWahid Hamid
Hendon, London

Rajab 1418/November 1997

Note on Qur'anic Script

● A detailed note on Features of the Qur'anic Script is given at the beginning of the accompanying book *Selections from the Qur'an*. Readers may find it useful to refer to this at an early stage.

● In this Textbook, the hamzatu-l wasl on an alif (‍آ) is not shown in the Qur'anic text.

However, the hamzatu-l qat' with an alif (آ and إ) is always shown.

● Reference numbers for Qur'anic text is given throughout. For example, in the reference number 85: 21 - the 85 refers to the surah number and 21 refers to the ayah or verse number.

How to use this book

1. You should be able to read and write the Arabic script before using this book. If you can't, use the *MELS Easy Steps in Arabic* course which includes (1) *Easy Steps in Qur'an Reading* with accompanying audiocassette tapes and (2) *Easy Steps in Arabic Handwriting (Workbooks 1 & 2)*. This course can be completed in 2-3 weeks or about 25 hours of study and practice.

The Al-Qari software on CD (PC & Mac formats) for reading the Arabic script, produced by SoundVision in Chicago, is excellent for self study.

For features of the Qur'anic Arabic script, see the Note at the beginning of the **Selections** book.

2. Read the Basic Word List 1. This contains words which, including their derivatives, occur more than 100 times in the Qur'an.

Learn these words and their meanings as soon as possible.

Return to the list frequently to revise and test yourself.

Use this Word List as a reference.

You do not have to learn all the words by heart before proceeding, but the quicker you memorize them, the faster you will get through the Units of the book.

3. Each Unit is made up of two facing pages and contains:

  - on the left page, step by step explanations of the grammar and structure of Arabic. Study this carefully.

  - on the facing page, selected Qur'anic text giving examples of the points of grammar and Arabic structure covered on the left page. Each of these pages has 15 lines of Qur'anic text. A small solid square ■ next to a line of text shows there is a relevant note at the bottom of the page.

  • Make sure you can read the Arabic fluently.

  • Listen to the recording of the text and its meaning on the cassette - one page only at a time.

  • Read the text aloud several times.

  • Revise the material on the left page.

  • Test your understanding of the text by covering the English translation and attempt a translation of the Arabic text.

  • Practice copying the Arabic text to gain fluency in writing and as an aid to memorizing.

4. Do the exercises for the Unit you are studying in the accompanying Workbook.

5. Ideally, go to the next Unit only when you have mastered the material in the preceding Unit(s).

6. However, you can press on, while continually revising previous Units and the Word List.

7. When you have finished Section Two, you could **start learning Word List 2** which contains words which, with their derivatives, occur between 50 and 100 times in the Qur'an.

8. When you have finished Section 3, you could **start learning Word List 3** which contains words which, with their derivatives, occur between 25 and 49 times in the Qur'an.

9. Once you have started on the course, you may find it helpful to listen to the **Qur'anic Selections** on the audiocassettes. These Selections contain many of the words in the basic word lists and points of grammar and structure covered.

10. Aim to read the Selections fluently and memorize as much as possible. At the end of the course you should be able to **understand much of what you read, in sha Allah.**

Transliteration of Arabic into English
An underlined vowel a, i and u indicates a long vowel in the Arabic:
kit<u>a</u>b = kitaab; kar<u>i</u>m = kariim;
ras<u>u</u>l = rasuul

Abbreviations used in this Textbook
m. masculine; f. feminine;
s. singular; d. dual;   p. plural

When referring to pronouns and verbs:
1. 1st person - the person speaking - **I, we**
2. 2nd person - the person spoken to - **you**
3. 3rd person - the person spoken about - **he, she, they**

e.g.
3.f.s.   = 3rd person feminine singular = **she**
3.m.d. = 3rd person masculine dual = **they two**
2.m.p. = 2nd person masculine plural = **you**
1.m. & f. s. = 1st person masculine and feminine singular = **I**

act. part.	active participle
pass. part.	passive participle
nom.	nominative
acc.	accusative
gen.	genitive
prep.	preposition
lit.	literally

Word List 1

The following list contains words which occur frequently in the Qur'an. It is arranged in Arabic alphabetical order.

This word list is placed at the beginning of the book for easy reference. You are not expected to memorize all the words at this stage but the sooner you do so the easier it would be to progress quickly. This is because these are the main words used throughout the book.

In the list, many words are first given in their simplest form. This form is a verb which is usually made up of three letters and which has the meaning of **he + the past tense.** For example:

خَلَقَ   **He created.**

This form is called the **root word** or the **root** from which other words are derived or formed. In general, these other derived words are not all included in this list.[1] Most root words in the list, in addition to the words derived from them, occur **more than 100 times** in the Qur'an.

In Arabic, it is helpful to learn the past tense of a verb together with its present form, for example:

خَلَقَ / يَخْلُقُ   **He created/He creates.** [2]

The plural of some nouns is given after the stroke /, for example:

قَلْبٌ / قُلُوبٌ   **heart/hearts.**   أَبٌ / ءَابَاءٌ   **father, ancestor/pl.**

The definite article اَلْ   **the**, is put before some nouns, for example:

اَلْأَرْضُ **the earth.**

You will find it helpful to return to this Basic Word List frequently. Read it aloud often, and memorize it as quickly as possible.

---

(1) In the Word Lists, Roman numerals from II to X are used for verbs derived from the root. For the significance of these Roman numerals see Section 5 of this book.

(2) Instead of writing out in full 'He created/He creates', dictionaries simply use the English infinitive 'to create' . This is only for convenience. In this and the other two Word Lists at the end of this book, the infinitive will be used when giving the meaning of an Arabic verb. e.g.:

جَعَلَ / يَجْعَلُ   **to make**   (instead of 'he made/he makes').

● **Read this Word List aloud often, and memorize it as quickly as possible.**

أَهْلٌ	family
أُوْلَـٰئِكَ (أولاء + ك)	those
ءَايَةٌ / ءَايَاتٌ	verse, sign, message/pl.

ا

أَبٌ / ءَابَاءٌ	father, ancestor/pl.
أَتَى / يَأْتِى	to come
أَجْرٌ / أُجُورٌ	reward/rewards
أَخَذَ / يَأْخُذُ	to take
اتَّخَذَ / يَتَّخِذُ	VIII. to adopt; to take
اَلأَخِرَةُ	the Hereafter
اَلأَخِرُ	last
ءَاخِرُ / ءَاخِرُونَ	other/others
أُخْرَى	other (f)
اَلأَرْضُ	the earth
أَكَلَ / يَأْكُلُ	to eat
أَلِيمٌ	painful
إِلَـٰهٌ / ءَالِهَةٌ	god, object of worship
اَللَّهُ	Allah, God
أَمَرَ / يَأْمُرُ	to command
أَمْرٌ / أُمُورٌ	matter, thing; order/pl.
أَمِنَ / يَأْمَنُ	to be secure
أَمِينٌ	trustworthy, secure
ءَامَنَ / يُؤْمِنُ	IV. to believe
مُؤْمِنٌ / مُؤْمِنُونَ	believer/believers (m.)
مُؤْمِنَةٌ / مُؤْمِنَاتٌ	believer/believers (f.)
إِيمَانٌ	faith, belief
إِنْسٌ	mankind, man
إِنْسَانٌ	human being
نَاسٌ	mankind, people

ت

بَصُرَ / يَبْصُرُ	to see, to perceive
بَصَرٌ / أَبْصَارٌ	sight
بَصِيرٌ	All-Seeing, Aware (attribute of God)
بَعْدَ	after
بَعِيدٌ	far
بُعْدًا لِ	away with!
بَعْضٌ	some
بَيَّنَ / يُبَيِّنُ	II. to clarify, announce
بَيِّنَاتٌ	clear teachings; pronouncements
مُبِينٌ	clear, plain, obvious
بَيْنَ	between, among
اِبْنٌ / بَنُونَ / أَبْنَاءٌ	son/sons - children
بَنِينَ	children/acc. & gen.
اِبْنَةٌ / بَنَاتٌ	daughter/daughters

ت

تَبِعَ	to follow
اتَّبَعَ / يَتَّبِعُ	VIII. to follow; adopt

ج

جَزَى / يَجْزِى	to reward, recompense
جَزَاءٌ	reward, recompense
جَعَلَ / يَجْعَلُ	to make; appoint
جَمَعَ / يَجْمَعُ	to gather
جَمِيعًا	together
أَجْمَعِين	all together
جَنَّةٌ / جَنَّاتٌ	garden/gardens
الْجَنَّةُ	Paradise, the Garden
جَاءَ / يَجِىءُ	to come

ح

حَتَّى	until
حَسِبَ / يَحْسَبُ	to reckon, think
حِسَابٌ	account, reckoning
حَسُنَ	to be good
حَسَنَةٌ / حَسَنَاتٌ	a good deed/pl.
أَحْسَنُ	better
أَحْسَنَ / يُحْسِنُ	IV. to do good
مُحْسِنٌ / مُحْسِنُونَ	(act. part. of IV.) doer of good
حَقٌّ	truth; right
اَلْحَقُّ	the Truth, Reality (also an attribute of God)
أَحَقُّ	more deserving
حَكَمَ / يَحْكُمُ	to judge
حُكْمٌ	a law, ruling
حِكْمَةٌ	wisdom

اَلْحَكِيمُ	the Most Wise (attribute of God)
حَىَّ / يَحْيَى	to live
أَحْيَا / يُحْيِى	IV. to give life, to bring into life
حَىٌّ / أَحْيَاءُ	a living being/living beings
اَلْحَىُّ	The Ever-Living (attribute of God)
حَيَاةٌ	life

خ

خَرَجَ / يَخْرُجُ	to go out, leave
خُرُوجٌ	going out, leaving; exit
أَخْرَجَ / يُخْرِجُ	IV. to bring forth, produce
إِخْرَاجٌ	producing; expulsion
خَلَفَ / يَخْلُفُ	to be behind
خَلْفَ	behind
خَلَّفَ / يُخَلِّفُ	II. to appoint as successor; to leave behind
خَالَفَ / يُخَالِفُ	III. to disagree; to disobey
اخْتَلَفَ / يَخْتَلِفُ	VIII. to disagree
اخْتِلَافٌ	disagreement
اسْتَخْلَفَ / يَسْتَخْلِفُ	X. to appoint as successor
خَلَقَ / يَخْلُقُ	to create
خَلْقٌ	creation
خَالِقٌ	Creator
اَلْخَالِقُ	the Creator (attribute of God)
خَافَ / يَخَافُ	to be afraid
خَوْفٌ	fear

خَيْرٌ	better	رَأْىٌ	a sighting; opinion
خَيْرٌ مِنْ	better than	آرَى / يُرِى	IV. to show
خَيْرَاتٌ	good deeds; charity	رِيَاءٌ	ostentation
		رَبٌّ	Lord, Sustainer

د

دَخَلَ / يَدْخُلُ	to enter	رَجَعَ / يَرْجِعُ	to return
أَدْخَلَ / يُدْخِلُ	IV. to cause to enter; to admit	مَرْجِعٌ	a return
دَعَا / يَدْعُو	to call upon someone, supplicate; to invite	رَحِمَ / يَرْحَمُ	to be merciful
دُعَاءٌ / أَدْعِيَاءُ	supplication/pl.	رَحْمَةٌ	mercy
الدُّنْيَا	the world	الرَّحْمـٰنُ	The Most Gracious (attribute of God)
حَيَاةُ الدُّنْيَا	the life of this world	الرَّحِيمُ	The Most Merciful (attribute of God)
دُونَ	without	أَرْحَامٌ	wombs
الدِّينُ	religion; the true faith; judgment	رَزَقَ / يَرْزُقُ	to provide (sustenance)
دَيْنٌ	a debt	رِزْقٌ	sustenance
		الرَّزَّاقُ	The Provider, Sustainer (attribute of God)

ذ

ذَكَرَ / يَذْكُرُ	to mention; to remember	أَرْسَلَ / يُرْسِلُ	IV. to send
ذَكَّرَ / يُذَكِّرُ	II. to remind	مُرْسَلٌ / مُرْسَلُونَ	(pass. part.) messenger
ذِكْرٌ	mentioning; a reminder, remembrance	رَسُولٌ / رُسُلٌ	messenger, messengers
تَذَكَّرَ / يَتَذَكَّرُ	V. to remind oneself	رِسَالَةٌ / رِسَالَاتٌ	message, messages
ذَكَرٌ / ذُكُورٌ	male, males	أَرَادَ / يُرِيدُ	IV. to want
ذُو / ذَا / ذِى	(nom./acc./gen.) possessor		

س

		سَأَلَ / يَسْأَلُ	to ask
		سُؤَالٌ	a question

ر

		سَائِلٌ / سَائِلُونَ	(act. part.) a questioner/pl.
رَأَى / يَرَى	to see	مَسْؤُولٌ / مَسْؤُولُونَ	(pass. part.) questioned; a responsible person/pl.
		تَسَاءَلَ / يَتَسَاءَلُ	VI. to ask one another

سَبِيلٌ / سُبُلٌ	way, path (f)/pl.
أَسْلَمَ / يُسْلِمُ	IV. to submit
إِسْلَامٌ	submission
اَلْإِسْلَامُ	Islam
مُسْلِمٌ / مُسْلِمُونَ	(act. part.) one who submits. Muslim (m)/pl.
مُسْلِمَةٌ / مُسْلِمَاتٌ	(act. part.) one who submits (f) Muslimah/pl.
سَلَامٌ	peace
سَمِعَ / يَسْمَعُ	to hear
سَمْعٌ	hearing
السَّمِيعُ	The All Hearing (attribute of God)
اِسْتَمَعَ / يَسْتَمِعُ	VIII. to listen
مُسْتَمِعٌ / مُسْتَمِعُونَ	(act. part. of VIII.) a listener
سَمَاءٌ / سَمَـٰوَاتٌ	sky, heaven/pl.
سَاءَ / يَسُوءُ	to be evil, bad
سُوءٌ	evil
سَيِّئَةٌ / سَيِّئَاتٌ	evil deed/ evil deeds

ش

شَدَّ	to be strong
شَدِيدٌ	strong, severe
أَشَدُّ	stronger, more severe
أَشْرَكَ / يُشْرِكُ	IV. to associate (others with God)
شِرْكٌ	associating (others with God); polytheism, idolatry
شَرِيكٌ / شُرَكَاءُ	partner
مُشْرِكٌ / مُشْرِكُونَ	(act. part of IV; m.) one who associates, polytheist/pl.

مُشْرِكَةٌ / مُشْرِكَاتٌ	(act. part of IV. f.) polytheist, pl.
شَهِدَ / يَشْهَدُ	to witness
أَشْهَدَ / يُشْهِدُ	IV. to call as a witness
أُشْهِدَ	(passive) to die as a martyr
شَاهِدٌ / شَاهِدُونَ	a witness, witnesses
شَهِيدٌ / شُهَدَاءُ	witness, martyr/pl.
شَهَادَةٌ	testimony; martyrdom
شَاءَ / يَشَاءُ	to wish, to will
شَيْءٌ / أَشْيَاءُ	a thing, things

ص

صَبَرَ / يَصْبِرُ	to be patient, steadfast
صَبْرٌ	patience, steadfastness, courage
صَابِرٌ / صَابِرُونَ	a steadfast person (m)/pl.
صَابِرَةٌ / صَابِرَاتٌ	a steadfast person (f) /pl.
صَبَّارٌ	a very steadfast person
صَدَقَ / يَصْدُقُ	to be truthful, to speak the truth
صِدْقٌ	truthfulness
صَادِقٌ / صَادِقُونَ	a truthful person (m)/pl.
صَدَقَةٌ / صَدَقَاتٌ	an act of charity/pl.
صَلَحَ	to be good, righteous
أَصْلَحَ / يُصْلِحُ	IV. to set aright, reform
إِصْلَاحٌ	setting aright, reform
صَالِحٌ / صَالِحُونَ	a righteous person/pl.
الصَّالِحَاتُ	righteous deeds

ض

ضَلَّ / يَضِلُّ	to go astray
أَضَلَّ / يُضِلُّ	IV. to cause (someone) to go astray
ضَلَالٌ	going astray; error
ضَالٌّ / ضَالُّونَ	one who is astray/pl.
أَضَلُّ	more misguided, more astray

ط

طَاعَ / يَطِيعُ —	to obey
طَاعَةٌ	obedience
أَطَاعَ / يُطِيعُ	IV. to obey
اِسْتَطَاعَ / يَسْتَطِيعُ	X. to be able

ظ

ظَلَمَ / يَظْلِمُ	to be unjust, to wrong, to be tyrannical
ظُلْمٌ	injustice, tyranny
ظَالِمٌ / ظَالِمُونَ	an unjust person, tyrant, wrongdoer/pl.
أَظْلَمَ / يُظْلِمُ	IV. to injure; to become dark
ظُلُمَاتٌ	darkness (lit. darknesses)

ع

عَبَدَ / يَعْبُدُ	to worship
عَبْدٌ / عِبَادٌ ـ عَبِيدٌ	a servant/servants

عِبَادَةٌ	worship
اِعْتَدَى / يَعْتَدِى	VIII. to overstep; to commit an aggression, to violate
عَدَاوَةٌ	enmity
عَدُوٌّ / أَعْدَاءُ	an enemy
عَذَّبَ / يُعَذِّبُ	II. to punish
عَذَابٌ	punishment
الْعَزِيزُ	The Most Powerful (attribute of God)
عَظِيمٌ	great, magnificent, awesome
الْعَظِيمُ	The Most Great (attribute of God)
عَلِمَ / يَعْلَمُ	to know
عِلْمٌ	knowledge
عَالِمٌ / عَالِمُونَ ـ عُلَمَاءُ	(act. part) one who knows, scholar/pl.
أَعْلَمُ	more knowledgeable
مَعْلُومٌ	(pass. part) known
الْعَلِيمُ	The All-knowing (attribute of God)
عَلَّمَ / يُعَلِّمُ	II. to teach
تَعَلَّمَ / يَتَعَلَّمُ	V. to learn
عَلَى	(prep.) on, above; against; on account of; despite
عَمِلَ / يَعْمَلُ	to work, do
عَامِلٌ / عَامِلُونَ	(act. part.) working, worker/pl
عَمَلٌ / أَعْمَالٌ	deed, action/pl.
عِنْدَ	(prep.) at, with, beside (also to express possession)

غ

غَفَرَ / يَغْفِرُ	to forgive
اِسْتَغْفَرَ / يَسْتَغْفِرُ	X. to ask forgiveness
الغَفُورُ	The Forgiving (attribute of God)
الغَفَّارُ	The Most Forgiving (attribute of God)
غَيْرَ	not

ف

فَضَّلَ / يُفَضِّلُ	II. to prefer
فَضْلٌ	grace, bounty
فَعَلَ / يَفْعَلُ	to do, make
فِى	in, into, among, on

ق

قَبْلَ	before
قَتَلَ / يَقْتُلُ	to kill
قَتْلٌ	killing, murder
قَتَّلَ / يُقَتِّلُ	II. to massacre
تَقْتِيلٌ	a massacre
قَاتَلَ / يُقَاتِلُ	III. to fight
قِتَالٌ	fighting
اقْتَتَلَ / يَقْتَتِلُ	VIII. to quarrel
قَدَرَ / يَقْدِرُ	to be able
قَدَّرَ / يُقَدِّرُ	II. to determine
قَدْرٌ	power, destiny

القَدِيرُ	The All-Powerful (attribute of God)
قَلَّبَ / يُقَلِّبُ	II. to cause to turn; to make succeed in turns
قَلْبٌ / قُلُوبٌ	heart, hearts
انْقَلَبَ / يَنْقَلِبُ	VIII to be turned about or away from; to be overthrown
قَالَ / يَقُولُ	to say
قِيلَ	(passive) it was said
قَوْلٌ	a saying, speech
قَامَ / يَقُومُ	to stand
أَقَامَ / يُقِيمُ	IV. to establish, set up; to keep up
قِيَامٌ	standing, establishing
اِسْتَقَامَ / يَسْتَقِيمُ	X. to stand firm
مُسْتَقِيمٌ	straight
القِيَامَةُ	the Resurrection
قَوْمٌ	a people

ك

كَبُرَ	to be great, serious
كَبِيرٌ	big, great; old
أَكْبَرُ	bigger, greater, older
اسْتَكْبَرَ / يَسْتَكْبِرُ	X. to be proud, arrogant
اِسْتِكْبَارٌ	pride, arrogance
كَتَبَ / يَكْتُبُ	to write; prescribe
كِتَابٌ / كُتُبٌ	book, scripture/pl.
كَثُرَ	to be plentiful

كَثِيرٌ	much, many
أَكْثَرُ	more, most
كَذِبَ / يَكْذِبُ	to lie
كِذْبٌ	a lie
كَاذِبٌ / كَاذِبُونَ	(act. part.) liar, liars
كَذَّابٌ	a great liar
كَذَّبَ / يُكَذِّبُ	II. to deny, reject
مُكَذِّبُونَ	(act. part. pl. of II) those who deny
كَفَرَ / يَكْفُرُ	to disbelieve, to be ungrateful, to hide
كُفْرٌ	disbelief, rejection (of Truth)
كَافِرٌ / كَافِرُونَ ـ كُفَّارٌ	disbeliever/disbelievers
كَفَّرَ / يُكَفِّرُ	II. to atone; to wipe away (sin)
كُلٌّ	each, every
كَانَ / يَكُونُ	to be
مَكَانٌ	a place

ل

لِ	to, for
لَعَلَّ	perhaps
لَقِيَ / يَلْقَى	to meet
لِقَاءٌ	a meeting
أَلْقَى / يُلْقِى	IV. to throw; to receive
تَلَقَّى / يَتَلَقَّى	V. to get, obtain
الْتَقَى / يَلْتَقِى	VIII. to encounter

م

مَا	what, whatever; not
مَتَى	when
مَثَلٌ / أَمْثَالٌ	an example, likeness, comparison, parable
مِثْلَ	like
مَعَ	with
مَلَكَ / يَمْلِكُ	to own; to control
مُلْكٌ	dominion, sovereignty
الْمَلِكُ	The Owner, the Sovereign (attribute of God)
مَلَكٌ	an angel
الْمَلَائِكَةُ	the angels
مِنْ	from
مَنْ	who, whoever
مَاتَ / يَمُوتُ	to die
مَوْتٌ	death
مَيِّتٌ / أَمْوَاتٌ	dead, dead person/pl.
مَيِّتٌ / مَيِّتُونَ ـ مَوْتَى	dead, dead person/pl.

ن

نَبَأٌ / أَنْبَاءٌ	news/pl.
نَبِيٌّ / نَبِيُّونَ ـ أَنْبِيَاءُ	a prophet/ prophets
النَّبِيُّ	the Prophet
النُّبُوَّةُ	prophethood
أَنْذَرَ / يُنْذِرُ	IV. to warn
نَذِيرٌ	a warner
مُنْذِرٌ / مُنْذِرُونَ	(act. part. of IV.) warner/pl.

نَزَلَ / يَنْزِلُ	to descend
نَزَّلَ / يُنَزِّلُ	II. to send down, reveal
تَنْزِيلٌ	a revelation
أَنْزَلَ / يُنْزِلُ	to send down; to reveal; to bestow
نَصَرَ / يَنْصُرُ	to help
نَصْرٌ	help
نَاصِرٌ / نَاصِرُونَ	(act. part.) helper/pl.
أَنْصَارٌ	helpers
نَصِيرٌ	helper
نَظَرَ / يَنْظُرُ	to see, to look
انْتَظَرَ / يَنْتَظِرُ	VIII. to wait
نَفْسٌ / أَنْفُسٌ – نُفُوسٌ	self, person, soul/pl,
نَارٌ	fire
نُورٌ	light
مُنِيرٌ	light-giving, radiant
نَاسٌ	people, human beings, mankind

هـ

هَدَى / يَهْدِى	to guide
هُدًى	guidance
اهْتَدَى / يَهْتَدِى	VIII. to be guided
مُهْتَدٍ / مُهْتَدُونَ	(pass. part. of VIII.) one who is guided/pl.

و

وَجَدَ / يَجِدُ	to find
وَعَدَ / يَعِدُ	to promise

وَعْدٌ	a promise
وَلَدَ / يَلِدُ	to beget; to reproduce
وَلَدَت	she gave birth
وَالِدٌ	(act. part. m.) father
وَالِدَةٌ	(act. part. f.) mother
وَالِدَانِ / وَالِدَينِ	(dual) parents
وَلَدٌ / أَوْلَادٌ	child, boy/children
وَقَى	to guard, protect
اتَّقَى / يَـتَّقِى	VIII. to be careful, wary; to be conscious (of God); to fear (God)
مُتَّقٍ / مُتَّقُونَ	one who is wary, conscious (of God); a God-conscious person
تَقْوَى	God-consciousness, piety; fear (of God)

ي

يَدٌ / أَيْدِى	hand/hands
يَسَّرَ / يُـيَسِّرُ	II. to make easy, facilitate
يَمِينٌ	right; right hand; an oath
أَيْمَانٌ	oaths
مَيْمَنَةٌ	right hand
يَوْمٌ / أَيَّامٌ	day, aeon/days, aeons
يَوْمَئِذٍ	on that day

Unit 1

Nouns, pronouns and adjectives: masculine

فَصَبْرٌ جَمِيلٌ

Sabr **is beautiful**
We translate the word *sabr* as 'patience' in line 15 opposite. However, sabr has a much wider meaning. It has the sense of courage, firmness, endurance and perseverance. Sabr is mentioned many times in the Qur'an. It is an important quality of a believer in God.

In Arabic, there are only two genders - masculine and feminine.

Masculine

Nouns

The three nouns below are all masculine.

رَجُلٌ a man   كِتَابٌ a book   أَمْرٌ a command

In English, *a* or *an* is called the indefinite article; it is written separately from the word to which it refers. You will notice that there is no separate word for *a* or *an* in Arabic. The tanwin ٌ at the end of the three words above tells us that we are referring to **a** man , **a** book, **a** command.

Pronouns

If we speak **about** any of the above nouns, we use the pronoun هُوَ meaning 'he'.

In Arabic we can combine the pronoun هُوَ with each of the above nouns to form a complete sentence.

1. هُوَ رَجُلٌ   He is a man. NQ

2. هُوَ كِتَابٌ   It is a book. NQ

3. هُوَ أَمْرٌ   It is a command. NQ

Notice in sentences 2 and 3 above, we use the word 'it' to translate هُوَ . In English we cannot say 'He is a book' or 'He is a command'. In Arabic we can. هُوَ **can be a person, a thing or an idea.**

Also in the above, there is no word for 'is' in Arabic. We often have to add the word 'is' (or 'are', 'am', 'was', 'were' or other parts of the verb 'to be') when we translate from Arabic to English.

We can also use the word هَـٰذَا **this** or ذَٰلِكَ **that** with the above words to form complete sentences.

هَـٰذَا رَجُلٌ This is a man. NQ   ذَٰلِكَ رَجُلٌ That is a man. NQ

هَـٰذَا كِتَابٌ This is a book. NQ   ذَٰلِكَ كِتَابٌ That is a book. NQ

هَـٰذَا أَمْرٌ This is a command. NQ   ذَٰلِكَ أَمْرٌ That is a command. NQ

Adjectives

In line 2 opposite, the noun قُرْءَانٌ has an adjective مَجِيدٌ .

In Arabic, the adjective follows its noun and must agree with it.

The noun قُرْءَانٌ is singular, masculine and ends with tanwin ٌ ;   its adjective مَجِيدٌ must also be singular, masculine and end with tanwin ٌ .

(You can tell whether a word is masculine or feminine when you study Unit 2.)

In lines 3, 5, 9 and 11 opposite, each noun has an adjective. Notice how each adjective agrees with its noun:

قُرْءَانٌ كَرِيمٌ   a noble Qur'an

ذِكْرٌ مُبَارَكٌ   a blessed reminder

إِلَـٰهٌ وَاحِدٌ   one God

صِرَاطٌ مُسْتَقِيمٌ   a straight way

English	#	Arabic		Glossary
It is a Qur'an. 85: 21	1	هُوَ قُرْءَانٌ		
It is a glorious Qur'an. 85: 21	2	هُوَ قُرْءَانٌ مَجِيدٌ		
Indeed, it is a noble Qur'an. 56: 77	3 ■	إِنَّهُ لَقُرْءَانٌ كَرِيمٌ		
This is a reminder. 21: 24	4	هَـٰذَا ذِكْرٌ		
This is a blessed reminder. 21: 50	5	هَـٰذَا ذِكْرٌ مُبَارَكٌ		
This is only a human being. 23: 24	6 ■	مَا هَـٰذَا إِلَّا بَشَرٌ	مَا not	
He (was) only a servant. 43: 59	7 ■	إِنْ هُوَ إِلَّا عَبْدٌ	إِنْ not	
			إِلَّا except, but	
He is a believer. 20: 112	8	هُوَ مُؤْمِنٌ	بَشَر human being	
He is One God. 6: 19	9	هُوَ إِلَـٰهٌ وَاحِدٌ	جَمِيل beautiful	
This is a way. 19: 36	10	هَـٰذَا صِرَاطٌ		
This is a straight way. 19: 36	11	هَـٰذَا صِرَاطٌ مُسْتَقِيمٌ		
This is a day. 11: 77	12	هَـٰذَا يَوْمٌ		
That is a day. 11: 103	13	ذَٰلِكَ يَوْمٌ		
That is the Book. 2: 2	14 ■	ذَٰلِكَ الْكِتَابُ		
So, patience is beautiful. 12: 84	15 ■	فَصَبْرٌ جَمِيلٌ		

Notes for text above

■ *Line 3:* Many sentences without a verb in Arabic begin with the particle إِنَّ which may be translated as 'surely' or 'indeed'. The ـهُ attached to إِنَّ stands for هُوَ . إِنَّهُ may be translated as 'Indeed he' or 'Indeed it' - or simply as 'He is' or 'It is'. • Prefixed to (or added before) the word قُرْءَان is the letter لَـ . This لَـ is called 'the lam of emphasis'.

■ *Lines 6 & 7:* Here the word مَا means 'not'. The particle إِنْ also significes 'not' when followed by إِلَّا

which means 'except' or 'but'. مَا or إِنْ followed by إِلَّا has the sense of 'only', 'nothing but', 'no more than'. • The word عَبْد refers to the Prophet Jesus, peace be on him.

■ *Line 14:* The noun كِتَاب begins with the definite article الـ *the*. It ends with a single dammah. A word with الـ cannot have tanwin.

■ *Line 15:* The letter فَ is joined to صَبْر . فَ means 'and', 'and so' or 'therefore'.

Unit 2

Nouns, pronouns and adjectives: feminine

A **noun** is a name of any living being, object or idea.

A **pronoun** is a word used instead of a noun.

An **adjective** is a word which describes a noun.

The NQ sign shows that a sentence is not from the Qur'an.

The three nouns below are all feminine. They are feminine because they end with a ta' marbutah - ﺔ or ة :

اِمْرَأَةٌ a woman   جَنَّةٌ a garden   ءَايَةٌ a verse

If we speak **about** any of the above nouns, we use the pronoun هِيَ which means 'she'.

We can combine the pronoun هِيَ with each of the above nouns to form a complete sentence in Arabic.

1. هِيَ اِمْرَأَةٌ   She is a woman. NQ   2. هِيَ جَنَّةٌ   It is a garden. NQ

3. هِيَ ءَايَةٌ   It is a verse. NQ

Notice that in sentence 2 and 3 above we use the word 'it' to translate هِيَ . In English we cannot say 'She is a garden' or 'She is a verse'. In Arabic we can. هِيَ can refer to a person, a thing or an idea. (هِيَ can also mean '**they**' in Arabic when it refers to the plural of certain nouns. For an example, see line 15 opposite).

Again notice that there is no word for 'is' in the above Arabic sentences. And there is no separate word for '**a**' - you know why.

We can also use the feminine words هَـٰذِهِ *this*, and تِلْكَ *that*, with the above words to form complete sentences.

هَـٰذِهِ اِمْرَأَةٌ This is a woman. NQ   تِلْكَ اِمْرَأَةٌ That is a woman. NQ

هَـٰذِهِ جَنَّةٌ This is a garden. NQ   تِلْكَ جَنَّةٌ That is a garden. NQ

هَـٰذِهِ ءَايَةٌ This is a verse. NQ   تِلْكَ ءَايَةٌ That is a verse. NQ

Feminine words which do not end with ة .

In line 9 opposite, the word نَار *fire*, is feminine even though it does not end with a ة .

There are a few other words like this which are feminine:

(i) words which refer to females: أُمٌّ **a** mother   أُخْتٌ a sister

(ii) parts of the body which occur in pairs are usually feminine:

يَدٌ a hand   عَيْنٌ an eye   أُذُنٌ an ear   قَدَمٌ a foot

(iii) other words which have to be learnt individually:

شَـمْسٌ a sun   سَمَاءٌ sky, heaven   حَرْبٌ a war   نَفْسٌ a soul, person

سَبِيلٌ a way   الأَرْضُ the earth   جَهَنَّمُ hell   دَارٌ a house

Check the context

The word فِتْنَةٌ in line 1 opposite means 'a test' or 'a trial' in the verse quoted. However, the word فِتْنَةٌ has a wide variety of meanings. In popular usage, it is often used to mean trouble, discord or dissension. In the Qur'an, it is used in the sense of oppression and persecution (2: 191) where it is described as 'worse than killing'. It is also used in the sense of 'confusion' (3: 7), 'temptation' (4: 91) and 'harm' (5: 71). Check the context in which a word is used to determine its meaning.

Harder than stone
In line 15 opposite, the word هِيَ refers to

قُلُوب or 'hearts'. God says that some peoples' hearts do become like stone or even harder. Water gushes out from rocks but nothing good, like truth or compassion, comes from a hardened human heart.

18 *Access to Qur'anic Arabic* ◆ TEXTBOOK

It is a test. 39: 50	1	هِيَ فِتْنَةٌ
It (was) deserted. 2: 258	2	هِيَ خَاوِيَةٌ
It is a word. 23: 100	3 ■	إِنَّهَا كَلِمَةٌ
It is a tree. 37: 64	4 ■	إِنَّهَا شَجَرَةٌ
It is a cow. 2: 67	5 ■	إِنَّهَا بَقَرَةٌ
And indeed Paradise–it is the abode.79: 41	6 ■	فَإِنَّ الْجَنَّةَ هِيَ الْمَأْوَى
Indeed, this is a reminder. 73: 19	7	إِنَّ هَـٰذِهِ تَذْكِرَةٌ
This is Jahannam. 36: 64	8	هَـٰذِهِ جَهَنَّمُ
This is the fire. 52: 14	9	هَـٰذِهِ النَّارُ
This is my way. 12: 108	10	هَـٰذِهِ سَبِيلِي
That (was) a nation. 2: 134	11	تِلْكَ أُمَّةٌ
That (was) a favour. 26: 22	12	تِلْكَ نِعْمَةٌ
That is the Paradise. 19: 63	13	تِلْكَ الْجَنَّةُ
It is a snake. 20: 20	14	هِيَ حَيَّةٌ
And so, they (are) like stone. 2: 174	15 ■	فَهِيَ كَالْحِجَارَةِ

كَلِمَةٌ a word
شَجَرَةٌ a tree
بَقَرَةٌ a cow
مَأْوَى abode
نِعْمَةٌ a favour
حَيَّةٌ a snake
حِجَارَةٌ stone

Notes for text above

■ *Lines 3, 4 and 5:* إِنَّ and إِنَّهَا — the هَا attached to إِنَّ stands for هِيَ . إِنَّهَا may be translated simply as 'she is' or 'it is'.

■ *Line 6:* The word الْجَنَّةَ ends with a fat-hah because it is controlled by إِنَّ . A فَ is joined to the إِنَّ .

■ *Line 8:* The word جَهَنَّمُ ends with a single dammah; it does not take tanwin. Some nouns

referring to places and the names of people do not take tanwin.

■ *Line 15:* Here, the word هِيَ means 'they' and refers to قُلُوب hearts, which is mentioned earlier in the verse.

• The letter كَ attached to the alif of the definite article الـ , means 'like'. كَ causes the word حِجَارَةٍ to end in a kasrah.

Unit 3

Nouns, pronouns and adjectives: indefinite

In English, an adjective comes before its noun.
In Arabic, an adjective comes after its noun.

Singular and indefinite

1. رَسُولٌ كَرِيمٌ a noble messenger   2. وَعْدًا مَفْعُولاً a fulfilled promise

3. ءَايَةٍ بَيِّنَةٍ a clear sign

Nominative:

An adjective must always agree with its noun. In example 1 above, the noun رَسُولٌ is masculine and indefinite so the adjective كَرِيمٌ *noble*, must also be masculine and indefinite. The noun ends in tanwin ٌ , so the adjective also ends with tanwin ٌ . Nouns and adjectives ending with tanwin ٌ are said to be in the **nominative case** (Arabic: مَرْفُوع).

A noun is in the nominative case when :

i. it is the subject of a sentence: in line 5 opposite, رَسُولٌ كَرِيمٌ is the subject of the sentence. (For further notes on what is the subject of a sentence, see Unit 12.)

ii. it is the *mubtada* or first part of a simple sentence, e.g. عَبْدٌ in line 11.

iii. it is a complement in simple sentences, like عَذَابٌ in line 2. (A complement gives some information (*khabar*) about the first part of a sentence.)

Accusative

In example 2 above , both the noun and its adjective are masculine and indefinite. The noun وَعْدًا ends with tanwin اً. Notice there is an added alif after the tanwin ً .
The adjective مَفْعُولاً must also agree with its noun and end with tanwin اً and an alif. Nouns and adjectives with the ending اً are said to be in the **accusative case** (Arabic: مَنْصُوب). A noun is in the accusative case :

i. when it is controlled by particles like إِنَّ *indeed*, أَنَّ *that*, and لَكِنَّ *but*. For example, see the word اللَّهَ in line 8. For more examples, see Unit 9.

ii. when it is the object of a sentence. In line 10 opposite, the object of the sentence is نَفْسًا زَكِيَّةً , *an innocent person*. (Remember the word نَفْسًا is feminine although it does not end with a ة ; its adjective زَكِيَّةً must be feminine (with the ـة ending) to agree with it.
Note: The ـة with tanwin ً is not followed by an alif.)

iii. when it is used as an adverb. In line 9 opposite, لَيْلاً is accusative because it ends with tanwin ً and may be translated as '**by** *night*'. نَهَارًا is also accusative and may be translated as '**by** *day*'.

Genitive

In example 3 above, both the noun and its adjective are feminine and indefinite. (How do we know they are feminine?) The noun ءَايَةٍ ends with tanwin ٍ and so does its adjective. Nouns and adjectives ending with the tanwin ٍ are said to be in the **genitive case** (Arabic: مَجْرُور).

A noun is in the genitive case:

i. when it is controlled by a preposition such as عَلَى *on*, فِى *in*.

ii. to show possession. In line 15 opposite, the word رَسُولٍ is genitive and means '*of* a messenger'. The adjective كَرِيمٍ *noble*, is genitive to agree with its noun.

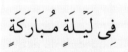

This is a strange thing. 50: 2	هَـٰذَا شَـىْءٌ عَجِيبٌ	1
This is a painful punishment. 44: 11	هَـٰذَا عَذَابٌ أَلِيمٌ	2
A blazing fire. 101: 11	نَارٌ حَامِيَةٌ	3
(It is) a good land and a forgiving Sustainer. 34: 15	بَلْدَةٌ طَيِّبَةٌ وَ رَبٌّ غَفُورٌ	4
A noble messenger has come to you. 44: 17	جَاءَكُمْ رَسُولٌ كَرِيمٌ	5 ■
For him (shall be) a generous reward. 57: 11	لَهُ أَجْرٌ كَرِيمٌ	6
And He prepared for them a generous reward. 33: 44	وَأَعَدَّ لَهُمْ أَجْرًا كَرِيمًا	7
Indeed, God is Forgiving, Merciful. 2:173	إِنَّ اللهَ غَفُورٌ رَحِيمٌ	8
By night and by day. 71: 5	لَيْلًا وَنَهَارًا	9
Have you killed an innocent person? 18: 74	أَقَتَلْتَ نَفْسًا زَكِيَّةً	10
And surely a believing servant (m.) is better than a polytheist. 2: 221	وَلَعَبْدٌ مُؤْمِنٌ خَيْرٌ مِنْ مُشْرِكٍ	11
And surely a believing servant (f.) is better than a polytheist. 2: 221	وَلَأَمَةٌ مُؤْمِنَةٌ خَيْرٌ مِنْ مُشْرِكَةٍ	12
And he is on a straight way. 16: 76	وَهُوَ عَلَى صِرَاطٍ مُسْتَقِيمٍ	13 ■
On a blessed night. 44: 3	فِى لَيْلَةٍ مُبَارَكَةٍ	14 ■
Indeed it is the speech of a noble messenger. 69: 40	إِنَّهُ لَقَوْلُ رَسُولٍ كَرِيمٍ	15 ■

to, for	لَ
him	ـهُ
them	هُمْ
he prepared	أَعَدَّ
you killed	قَتَلْتَ
begins a question	أَ

Notes for text above

■ *Line 5:* This sentence begins with a verb. جَاءَكُمْ means 'he has come to you'.

■ *Line 13:* The word صِرَاطٍ a path, is singular and masculine. It also ends with tanwin ـٍ and so it is genitive and indefinite. It is genitive because it is controlled by the preposition عَلَى on. The adjective مُسْتَقِيمٍ straight, is masculine and genitive because it must agree with its noun صِرَاطٍ.

■ *Line 14:* The word لَيْلَةٍ a night, is feminine. It also ends with tanwin ـٍ and so is genitive and indefinite. It is genitive because it is controlled by the preposition فِى in. The adjective مُبَارَكَةٍ blessed, is feminine and genitive because it must agree with its noun لَيْلَةٍ.

■ *Line 15:* رَسُولٍ is genitive because it shows possession - 'of a messenger'. The adjective كَرِيمٍ noble, is genitive to agree with its noun رَسُولٍ.

Nouns which end with tanwin are indefinite.

A word becomes definite when the definite article اَلْ is attached before it. اَلْ is always attached to the word which follows:

مَائِدَةٌ   a table   كِتَابٌ   a book

اَلْمَائِدَةُ   the table   اَلْكِتَابُ   the book

When a word is definite, it loses the 'n' of the tanwin.

When the word to which the اَلْ is attached begins with a 'sun' letter, the ل of the definite article loses its sukun and the sun letter gets a shaddah. This means that the ل of the definite article is omitted in pronunciation, and the sun letter is clearly doubled, e.g. الشَّمْسُ , *the sun*.

The sun letters are fourteen:

ت ث د ذ ر ز س ش ص ض ط ظ ل ن

Masculine, singular and definite
If a noun is masculine, singular and definite, its adjective must also be masculine, singular and definite. The adjective must also agree with its noun by having the same case endings. Study the following examples:

1.   اَلْقُرْءَانُ الْعَظِيمُ   the great Qur'an   (nominative) - ending with dammah

2.   اَلصِّرَاطَ الْمُسْتَقِيمَ   the straight path   (accusative) - ending with fat-hah

3.   اَلشَّيْطَانِ الرَّجِيمِ   the rejected Satan   (genitive) - ending with kasrah

In example 1 above, the word اَلْقُرْءَانُ is masculine and singular. It is definite because it has the definite article اَلْ. It is also in the nominative case because it ends with a dammah.

The adjective الْعَظِيمُ agrees with its noun الْقُرْءَانُ by being masculine and singular. It also has the definite article and ends with a dammah.

In examples 2 and 3, see how each adjective agrees with its noun.

Feminine, singular and definite
If a noun is feminine, singular and definite, its adjective must also be feminine, singular and definite. The adjective must also agree with its noun by having the same case endings. Study the following examples:

4.   النَّفْسُ الْمُطْمَئِنَّةُ   the satisfied soul (nominative) - ending with dammah

5.   اَلدَّارَ الْأَخِرَةَ   the next abode (accusative) - ending with fat-hah

6.   اَلْمَوْعِظَةِ الْحَسَنَةِ   good advice (genitive) - ending with kasrah

In example 5 above, the word اَلدَّارَ is one of those few words which are feminine even though they do not have a ة ending. اَلدَّارَ is also singular and definite. It is also in the accusative case because it ends with a fat-hah.

The adjective الْأَخِرَةَ agrees with its noun اَلدَّارَ by being feminine with a ة ending, by being singular, and by being definite by having اَلْ. It also ends with a fat-hah.

See how each adjective agrees with its noun in examples 4 and 6 above.

Note: The word اَلدُّنْيَا (line 9 opposite) does not change. It has the same form for all cases.

A word with the definite article cannot have tanwin.

In phrases showing possession like كِتَابُ اللَّهِ which means 'the book **of** Allah', the word كِتَابُ is definite but it must not have the definite article. The word اللَّهِ with its genitive ending means 'of Allah' (see Unit 10).

Grace and mercy
God's rahmah or grace and mercy extends over everything. The attributes of God as Rahman - most Gracious, and Rahim - most Merciful, are repeated over and over again in the Qur'an. God is ever ready to forgive the errant but repentant soul and His attribute as Ghafur - Forgiving - is also repeated often in the Qur'an.

اَلْوَدُودُ - the Loving ,

is another attribute of Allah. It is mentioned once in the Qur'an and refers to God's all-embracing love.

Indeed God is Forgiving, Merciful. 2: 173	1 إِنَّ اللَّهَ غَفُورٌ رَحِيمٌ
He is the Forgiving, the Loving (God). 85: 14	2 هُوَ الْغَفُورُ الْوَدُودُ
That is the great favour. 42: 22	3 ذٰلِكَ هُوَ الْفَضْلُ الْكَبِيرُ
Guide us the straight way. 1: 6	4 ■ اهْدِنَا الصِّرَاطَ الْمُسْتَقِيمَ
They fear the painful punishment. 51: 37	5 ■ يَخَافُونَ الْعَذَابَ الْأَلِيمَ
It is tremendous news. 38: 67	6 هُوَ نَبَأٌ عَظِيمٌ
Concerning the awesome news. 78: 2	7 ■ عَنِ النَّبَإِ الْعَظِيمِ
And a sign for them is the dead earth. 36: 33	8 وَءَايَةٌ لَهُمُ الْأَرْضُ الْمَيْتَةُ
The worldly life is only a play and a pastime. 47: 36	9 ■ إِنَّمَا الْحَيَوٰةُ الدُّنْيَا لَعِبٌ وَلَهْوٌ
And the next abode is better. 7: 169	10 وَالدَّارُ الْأَخِرَةُ خَيْرٌ
Indeed the next abode - it is truly the life! 29: 64	11 ■ إِنَّ الدَّارَ الْأَخِرَةَ لَهِيَ الْحَيَوَانُ
Call to the way of your Sustainer with wisdom and good exhortation. 16: 125	12 أُدْعُ إِلَى سَبِيلِ رَبِّكَ بِالْحِكْمَةِ وَالْمَوْعِظَةِ الْحَسَنَةِ
Say: O disbelievers! 109: 1	13 ■ قُلْ يَا أَيُّهَا الْكَافِرُونَ
O tranquil soul! 89: 27	14 ■ يَا أَيَّتُهَا النَّفْسُ الْمُطْمَئِنَّةُ
By the fig and the olive and Mount Sinai and this secure land. 95: 1-2	15 ■ وَالتِّينِ وَالزَّيْتُونِ وَطُورِ سِينِينَ وَهٰذَا الْبَلَدِ الْأَمِينِ

Notes for text above

■ *Line 4:* اهْدِنَا means 'Guide us'.

■ *Line 5:* يَخَافُونَ means 'They fear'.

■ *Line 7:* عَنْ is a preposition and means 'about' or 'concerning'. It has a kasrah on the نْ to link it in pronunciation with the following word.

■ *Line 9:* إِنَّمَا means 'only'.

■ *Line 11:* لَهِيَ is the لَ of emphasis + هِيَ.

■ *Line 12:* The word أُدْعُ means 'Call' or 'Invite'.

■ *Lines 13 and 14:* The interjection يَا - O! is the simple and usual way of addressing someone. Here it is joined to another interjection أَيُّهَا - also meaning O! (masculine, for singular and plural) which is immediately followed by الـ. The feminine form, أَيَّتُهَا is also followed directly by the definite article.

■ *Line 15:* The first وَ and the other three separate waws in this line are used for making an oath (qasam). Each of these waws is known as the 'waw al-qasam', and the words controlled by it are in the genitive. Two more examples: وَالْعَصْرِ By Time! وَاللَّهِ by God!

Unit 5

Nouns, and adjectives: number

The noun هُدًى does not change - it has the same form in the indefinite for all case endings. With the definite article it becomes اَلْهُدَى and does not change its ending.

إِنَّ هُدَى اللَّهِ هُوَ الْهُدَى

Truly God's guidance - it is the (only true) guidance.

الْمُتَّقِينَ

The word muttaqin in line 10 opposite is left un-translated but in line11 is given as those who are 'God-conscious'. Muttaqin is sometimes translated as the pious, the righteous, those who ward off evil, those who fear God or those who are wary of God.
The basic meaning of muttaqin is those who are careful - careful about not overstepping the limits which God in His knowledge and wisdom has set for the guidance and success of human beings. The main purpose of the Qur'an - mentioned at its beginning (2: 2) - is 'guidance for the muttaqin':

هُدًى لِلْمُتَّقِينَ

Number

In English, a noun or pronoun may be singular or plural. Plural refers to more than one.

In Arabic, a noun or pronoun (as well as an adjective or a verb) may be singular, dual or plural. Dual refers to two of something. Plural refers to more than two.

Read the following from the right to the left:

Plural		Dual		Singular	
مُسْلِمُونَ/ مِينَ	Muslims	مُسْلِمَانِ/ يَنِ	two Muslims	مُسْلِمٌ	a Muslim
ءَايَاتٌ/ ءَايَاتٍ	verses	ءَايَتَانِ/ يَنِ	two verses	ءَايَةٌ	a verse
رِجَالٌ	men	رَجُلَانِ/ يَنِ	two men	رَجُلٌ	a man
هُمْ	they	هُمَا	they (both)	هُوَ	he
هُنَّ	they	هُمَا	they (both)	هِيَ	she
جَعَلُوا	they made	جَعَلَا	they both made	جَعَلَ	he made

Dual

The dual of nouns and adjectives is formed from the singular by adding ـَانِ for the nominative and ـَيْنِ for the accusative and genitive. The ـة at the end of a singular word is changed into a normal ـت to which the dual ending is attached. (For dual masculine, see below. For dual feminine, see the next Unit.)

Plurals

In Arabic, there are three types of plural:

1. Sound masculine plural **2.** Sound feminine plural **3.** Broken plural

Sound plurals are easy to form. They are so called because the singular forms remain intact or sound. To these are added set endings for masculine plurals and other set endings for feminine plurals. Sound plurals are sometimes called *external plurals.* مُسْلِمُونَ with the set ending ـُونَ is an example of a sound masculine plural.

Broken plurals are formed by breaking up the singular pattern by adding new vowels or letters before, in between or after the root letters. رِجَال is an example of a broken plural.

Some words may have both a sound plural and a broken plural.

There are word patterns which will help us to recognise and learn plurals of words in Arabic. (See Unit 39.) At this stage, it is better to learn the plural of each word with its singular.

Sound masculine plural and dual

	Plural	Dual	Singular
nominative	مُسْلِمُونَ	مُسْلِمَانِ	مُسْلِمٌ
accusative	مُسْلِمِينَ	مُسْلِمَيْنِ	مُسْلِمًا
genitive	مُسْلِمِينَ	مُسْلِمَيْنِ	مُسْلِمٍ

Look carefully at the endings of the words above and see what letters and vowels are added to form the dual and plural. Note that the accusative and genitive endings for the dual are the same. For the sound plurals, the accusative and genitive endings are the same.

He is a believer. 4: 24	1 هُوَ مُؤْمِنٌ
They are believers. 8: 4	2 هُمُ الْمُؤْمِنُونَ
And the disbelievers - they are the wrongdoers. 2: 254	3 وَالْكَافِرُونَ هُمُ الظَّالِمُونَ
Those - they are the successful ones. 2: 5	■ 4 أُولَـٰئِكَ هُمُ الْمُفْلِحُونَ
Those - they are the losers. 2: 27	■ 5 أُولَـٰئِكَ هُمُ الْخَاسِرُونَ
Indeed these are truly misguided. 83: 32	■ 6 إِنَّ هَـٰؤُلَاءِ لَضَالُّونَ
O my Sustainer! Indeed, these are a people who do not believe. 43: 88	■ 7 يَـارَبِّ إِنَّ هَـٰؤُلَاءِ قَوْمٌ لَا يُؤْمِنُونَ
Indeed, God loves the doers of good. 2: 195	8 إِنَّ اللَّهَ يُحِبُّ الْمُحْسِنِينَ
And I am not from the polytheists. 6: 79	■ 9 وَمَا أَنَا مِنَ الْمُشْرِكِينَ
And know that God is with the muttaqin. 2: 194	10 وَاعْلَمُوا أَنَّ اللَّهَ مَعَ الْمُتَّقِينَ
This (lit. that) is the book - there is no doubt in it ...	11 ذَٰلِكَ الْكِتَابُ لَا رَيْبَ فِيهِ
...(it is) a guidance for the God-conscious. 2: 2	12 هُدًى لِلْمُتَّقِينَ
And that is the reward of the doers of good. 39: 34	13 ذَٰلِكَ جَزَاءُ الْمُحْسِنِينَ
Indeed the hypocrites (shall be) in the lowest depth (of the fire). 4: 145	14 إِنَّ الْمُنَافِقِينَ فِي الدَّرْكِ الْأَسْفَلِ
They both (were) in the cave. 9: 40	15 هُمَا فِي الْغَارِ

those	أُولَـٰئِكَ
these	هَـٰؤُلَاءِ
they	هُمُّ
a people	قَوْمٌ
they believe	يُؤْمِنُونَ
he loves	يُحِبُّ
doubt	رَيْبَ

Notes for text above

For each of the plurals in the text above, you should be able to say which is nominative, which is accusative and which is genitive, and why.

Remember that a noun is accusative when it is controlled by particles like إِنَّ or when(see Unit 12) it is the object of a verb. For example, in line 14, الْمُنَافِقِينَ is accusative because it is controlled by إِنَّ. Some nouns are genitive because they are controlled

by a preposition such as مِنْ from, لِ for, or مَعَ with. A noun may also be genitive because it shows possession - see الْمُحْسِنِينَ in line 13.

■ *Lines 6 & 7:* أُولَـٰئِكَ those, is the plural both of ذَٰلِكَ and تِلْكَ.

■ *Lines 4 & 5:* هَـٰؤُلَاءِ these, is the plural of both هَـٰذَا and هَـٰذِهِ this.

■ *Line 9:* The مَا here means 'not'. This sentence is therefore called a negative sentence.

Sound feminine plurals. The plural of feminine nouns and adjectives are formed according to the following patterns. The dual is also included.

	Plural	Dual	Singular
nominative	مُسلِماتٌ	مُسلِمَتانِ	مُسلِمَةٌ
accusative	مُسلِماتٍ	مُسلِمَتَينِ	مُسلِمَةً
genitive	مُسلِماتٍ	مُسلِمَتَينِ	مُسلِمَةٍ

You would note that for the sound feminine plural, the ta' marbutah of the singular becomes ـَاتٌ in the nominative and ـَاتٍ in the accusative and genitive.

Broken Plurals. While sound masculine and feminine plurals are formed by changes to the endings of words, broken plurals are formed by changes within a word and sometimes by the addition of prefixes and suffixes as well. Examples:

Singular	أُمٌّ	نَفسٌ	عالِمٌ	قَلبٌ
Plural	أُمَّهاتٌ	أَنفُس/نُفوسٌ	عُلَماءُ	قُلوبٌ

Note: Broken plurals of nouns referring to non-rational beings or things are considered to be gramatically **feminine singular**. This means that:

i.   the adjective of such a broken plural noun will be feminine singular;

ii. the pronouns used to refer to a broken plural noun will be feminine singular;

iii. if the broken plural is the subject of a verb, the verb will be feminine singular.

Separate Pronouns. We have already introduced a few pronouns like هُوَ he, هِيَ she, هُمْ they. These are known as 'separate' pronouns.

Because pronouns occur frequently in the Qur'an, we give below a chart of all the 'separate' pronouns in Arabic. (Read from right to left.)

	Plural		Dual		Singular	
they	هُمْ	they both	هُمَا	he, it	هُوَ	3.m.
they	هُنَّ	they both	هُمَا	she, it	هِيَ	3.f.
you	أَنتُمْ	you both	أَنـتُمَا	you	أَنتَ	2.m.
you	أَنتُنَّ	you both	أَنـتُمَا	you	أَنتِ	2.f.
we	نَحنُ	we	نَحنُ	I	أَنَا	1.m.&f.

The pronouns in the first two lines of the chart are referred to as 'third person' pronouns. 'Third persons' in grammar refer to persons **spoken about**. Notice that there are three pronouns for 'they' in Arabic.

The pronouns in the second two lines of the chart are referred to as 'second person' pronouns. Second persons in grammar refer to persons **spoken to**. Notice that there are five pronouns for 'you' in Arabic.

The pronouns in the last line of the chart are referred to as 'first person' pronouns. First persons in grammar refer to **persons speaking**. Note that the final alif of أَنَا is there to distinguish it from similarly spelt words, and is not pronounced. So أَنَا is pronounced ana, not ana.

Broken plurals

Broken plurals are formed by changes within a word and sometimes by the addition of prefixes and suffixes as well.
While there are word patterns for various broken plurals, it is best at this stage to learn the plural of each word with its singular.

Mixed groups

If a pronoun refers to a mixed group of people, the masculine is used. This applies to nouns and verbs as well.

In the chart, 3.m. is short for 3rd person masculine; 3.f. is for third person feminine.

Ayatullah

In line 4 opposite, the word ayah is translated as 'a sign'.
The word ayah is also used to denote 'a verse' of the Qur'an. There are 6236 ayat or verses in the Qur'an. Each ayah is a Divine 'message'. The word ayah, in its singular and plural forms, occurs almost 400 times in the Qur'an.
The vast natural phenomena of creation are all described as ayat, signs or messages - for those who reflect and use their reason - which must lead to an affirmation of faith in the Creator. Each part of creation - however great or minute - including what is within the human being is an Ayatullah or sign of God.

And the believing men and the believing women are protectors of one another. 9: 71	١ ■	وَالْمُؤْمِنُونَ وَالْمُؤْمِنَاتُ بَعْضُهُمْ أَوْلِيَاءُ بَعْضٍ
God has promised the believing men and the believing women gardens. 9: 72	٢	وَعَدَ اللَّهُ الْمُؤْمِنِينَ وَالْمُؤْمِنَاتِ جَنَّاتٍ
Indeed, the men who submit and the women who submit and the believing men and the believing women ... 33: 35	٣	إِنَّ الْمُسْلِمِينَ وَالْمُسْلِمَاتِ وَالْمُؤْمِنِينَ وَالْمُؤْمِنَاتِ
Surely in that is a sign for the believers. 15: 77	٤ ■	إِنَّ فِى ذَٰلِكَ لَآيَةً لِّلْمُؤْمِنِينَ
Surely in the heavens and the earth are signs for the believers. 45: 3	٥	إِنَّ فِى السَّمَـٰوَاتِ وَالْأَرْضِ لَآيَاتٍ لِّلْمُؤْمِنِينَ
And We made the night and the day two signs. 17: 12	٦	وَجَعَلْنَا اللَّيْلَ وَالنَّهَارَ ءَايَتَيْنِ
And surely Paradise - it is the goal. 79: 4	٧	فَإِنَّ الْجَنَّةَ هِىَ الْمَأْوَى
The companions of Paradise - they are the triumphant ones. 59: 20	٨	أَصْحَابُ الْجَنَّةِ هُمُ الْفَائِزُونَ
Two gardens on (the) right and left. 34: 5	٩ ■	جَنَّتَانِ عَن يَمِينٍ وَشِمَالٍ
For them (shall be) gardens of bliss. 22: 56	١٠	لَهُمْ جَنَّاتُ النَّعِيمِ
Indeed the muttaqin (shall be) in gardens and in bliss. 52: 17	١١	إِنَّ الْمُتَّقِينَ فِى جَنَّاتٍ وَنَعِيمٍ
They are not their mothers. 58: 2	١٢	مَا هُنَّ أُمَّهَاتِهِمْ
You are Muslims (those who submit to God). 2: 132	١٣	أَنتُمْ مُسْلِمُونَ
They are a people. 51: 53	١٤	هُمْ قَوْمٌ
We are helpers of (the cause of) God. 3: 52	١٥	نَحْنُ أَنصَارُ اللَّهِ

Notes for text above

For each of the plurals in the text above, you should be able to say which is nominative, which is accusative and which is genitive, and why. There are two nouns in the dual.

■ *Line 1:* بَعْضُهُمْ أَوْلِيَاءُ بَعْضٍ lit. some of them are protectors of some.

■ *Line 4:* ءَايَةً is accusative because it is controlled by إِنَّ . Note the lam of emphasis.

The preposition لِ means 'to' or 'for'. The alif of الْ is dropped when preceded by لِ .

لِ + الْمُؤْمِنِينَ = لِلْمُؤْمِنِينَ

■ *Line 9:* The preposition عَن normally means 'concerning' but here means 'on'.

Unit 7
Attached Pronouns

In the last Unit, we introduced 'separate pronouns'. Besides these, there are pronouns which are attached to the ends of words as suffixes. They are called 'attached pronouns' or 'pronoun suffixes'.

> Attached pronouns come at the end of nouns, prepositions, verbs and various particles.

An attached pronoun may be:

1. a possessive pronoun, attached to the end of a noun, as in:

رَسُولُهُ ← ـهُ + رَسُول
his messenger   his   messenger

رَبُّهَا   هَا + رَبُّ
her Sustainer   her   Sustainer

2. attached to a preposition, as in:

مِنْهُ   ـهُ + مِنْ
from him   him   from

مِنْهَا   هَا + مِنْ
from her   her   from

3. attached to particles like إِنَّ as in: إِنَّهُ and إِنَّهَا .

4. the object of a verb, as in:

جَعَلَهُ   ـهُ + جَعَلَ
he made it   it   he made

Below is a chart with the attached pronouns or pronoun suffixes. Read from right to left.

Plural		Dual		Singular		
them, their	هُمْ / هِمْ	them both, their	هُمَا / هِمَا	him, his/ it, its	ـهُ / ـهِ / ـه / ه	3.m.
them, their	هُنَّ / هِنَّ	them both, their	هُمَا / هِمَا	her/ it, its	هَا	3.f.
you, your	كُمْ	you both, your	كُمَا	you, your	كَ	2.m.
you, your	كُنَّ	you both, your	كُمَا	you, your	كِ	2.f.
we, our	نَا			me, my	ـِي / ـِى / ـنِى	1.m. & f.

> **A garment metaphor**
>
> The word *libas* (line 12 opposite) is used in the Qur'an as a metaphor for marriage relationships. A garment serves three essential purposes: it protects and insulates a person from the elements and provides warmth and comfort; it is something of beauty and adornment; it safeguards privacy and morality. A garment is also the closest thing to one's body. A husband must be such a garment for his wife and a wife must be such a garment for her husband - protecting, beautifying, supporting, and being close.

Notice that attached pronouns in the third person (except هَا) have two different forms, e.g. ـهُ and ـهِ . The form having a dammah is used if the preceding vowel is a dammah or fathah, eg. رَبُّهُ , and رَبَّهُ .

The form having a kasrah is used if the preceding vowel is a kasrah or there is a preceding a sukun on a ya', e.g. رَبِّهِ , and عَلَيْهِ .

For the 1.m. & f. attached pronoun ـِى , the word to which the ى is attached must be made to end in a kasrah to which a vowelless ya' is added, e.g. رَبِّى - my Lord. The exception to this is words like (عَلَى + ى) عَلَىَّ where the ى with a fat-hah is used. The نِى form is used with verbs and after prepositions or particles ending with نْ , e.g. جَعَلَنِى - He made me; مِنْ + نِى = مِنِّى - from me.

English	#	Arabic
Indeed, you are the messenger of God. 63: 1	1	إِنَّكَ لَرَسُولُ اللَّهِ
Indeed you are His messenger. 63: 1	2	إِنَّكَ لَرَسُولُهُ
To Him (belongs) whatever is in the heavens and whatever is on earth. 42: 4	3	لَهُ مَا فِى السَّمٰوٰتِ وَمَا فِى الْأَرْضِ
He (was) in her house. 12: 23	4	هُوَ فِى بَيْتِهَا
You alone we worship. 1: 5	5	إِيَّاكَ نَعْبُدُ
(O Maryam!) Your Sustainer has made beneath you a rivulet. 19: 24	6	قَدْ جَعَلَ رَبُّكِ تَحْتَكِ سَرِيًّا
He said (to her): I am only the messenger of your Sustainer. 19: 19	7	قَالَ إِنَّمَا أَنَا رَسُولُ رَبِّكِ
My punishment - it is the painful punishment. 15: 50	8	عَذَابِى هُوَ الْعَذَابُ الْأَلِيمُ
Truly, I am from among those who submit. 41: 33	9	إِنَّنِى مِنَ الْمُسْلِمِينَ
I am the servant of God. 19: 30	10	إِنِّى عَبْدُ اللَّهِ
Truly I am to you both a sincere adviser. (lit. from the sincere advisers). 7: 21	11	إِنِّى لَكُمَا مِنَ النَّاصِحِينَ
They (your wives) are a garment for you and you are a garment for them. 2: 187	12	هُنَّ لِبَاسٌ لَكُمْ وَأَنْتُمْ لِبَاسٌ لَهُنَّ
To you your religion and to me, my religion. 109: 6	13	لَكُمْ دِينُكُمْ وَلِىَ دِينِ
Surely, we are with you. 2: 14	14	إِنَّا مَعَكُمْ
God is our Sustainer and your Sustainer. To us our deeds and to you your deeds. 42: 15	15	اللَّهُ رَبُّنَا وَرَبُّكُمْ لَنَا أَعْمَالُنَا وَلَكُمْ أَعْمَالُكُمْ

Side vocabulary:

a rivulet — سَرِيًّا
a sincere adviser. — نَاصِحٌ
a garment — لِبَاسٌ

Notes for text above

■ **Lines 1 & 2:** Note the 'lam of emphasis'.

■ **Line 5:** The particle إِيَّا : The pronoun كَ is attached to إِيَّا which gives emphasis to the pronoun, thus conveying the meaning of 'You alone'.

Other pronouns are attached to إِيَّا in the Qur'an: إِيَّاهُ , him alone; إِيَّاىَ , me alone; إِيَّاهُمْ them alone; إِيَّاكُمْ you too; إِيَّانَا we alone.

■ **Line 9 :** Surely I - إِنَّنِى is a combination of نِى and إِنَّ

■ **Line 10:** Surely I - إِنِّى is a contraction of نِى and إِنَّ .

■ **Line 13:** my religion - دِينِ is short for دِينِى . The pronoun ىِ is sometimes dropped at the end of other words; for example, my Sustainer - رَبِّ is short for رَبِّى .

■ **Line 14:** إِنَّ + نَا = إِنَّا .

Unit 8
Prepositions

We have already come across a few prepositions: عَلَى on; فِي in; عَنْ about. We have noted that a word controlled by a preposition is genitive.

This Unit lists more prepositions used in the Qur'an. Some prepositions may be translated in different ways. We need to look at the context in which a preposition is used to determine its exact meaning.

Attached prepositions

There are two prepositions which are single letters attached to the words they control:

لِ - to, belonging to, for;   بِ - by, with, in.

The letter كَ as, like - is not a preposition but acts like one.

for whoever	لِ + مَنْ = لِمَنْ	with a heart	بِ + قَلْب = بِقَلْبٍ
to people	لِ + اَلنَّاس = لِلنَّاس	with a pen	بِ + القَلَم = بِالقَلَم
for God	لِ + اللَّه = لِلَّه	in the name	بِ + اِسْم = بِسْمٍ

Note: the alif of the definite article اَلْ is omitted when it is preceded by لِ ,

for example: لِ + الرَّسُولِ = لِلرَّسُولِ and لِ + لنَّاسِ = لِلنَّاسِ .

If a word begins with a لَ , the whole of the definite article اَلْ is omitted,

for example: لِ + اَللَّيْل = لِلَّيْل

When used with an attached pronoun لِ becomes لَ,

for example: لَكُمْ ، لَكَ ، لَهَا ، لَهُ; exception لِى

Separate prepositions

إِلَى / إِلَيـ	to	خَلْفَ	behind	فِي	in, among
بَعْدَ	after	عَنْ	about, concerning	قَبْلَ	before
بَيْنَ	between	عَلَى / عَلَيـ	on, against	مَعَ	with
تَحْتَ	under	عِنْدَ	at, with	مِنْ	among
حَتَّى	until, even	فَوْقَ	above		

The prepositions لَ , مَعَ and عِنْدَ are used to indicate possession as well: لَهُ ، مَعَهُ and عِنْدَه can all mean 'he has'.

Some verbs in Arabic are followed by a particular preposition for which no translation in English is needed:

غَفَرَ لَهُ He forgave him (lit: he forgave to him).

اِسْتَعِذْ	Seek protection!
ءَامَنَّا	We believed
عِزَّة	honour
حَرَام	sacred, inviolable
الأَقْصَى	the further

A preposition is placed before a noun or pronoun. It tells you the position or place of something in either space or time.
Some prepositions in Arabic are used to show possession.

سَلَامٌ عَلَيْكُمْ

'Peace be upon you! Well have you done. Enter, then, this Paradise, herein to abide.' This will be the greeting of the keepers of Paradise to those who were conscious of their Creator, who were true to their nature and fulfilled their purpose on earth. Their response to the greeting of the keepers of Paradise will be: 'All praise is due to God, Who has made His promise to us come true...'

So, seek protection with God from the rejected Satan. 16: 98	1 ■ فَاسْتَعِذْ بِاللَّهِ مِنَ الشَّيْطَانِ الرَّجِيمِ
In the name of God, most Gracious, most Merciful. 1: 1	2 ■ بِسْمِ اللَّهِ الرَّحْمٰنِ الرَّحِيمِ
And among people are those who say, 'We have believed in God and the Last Day...'	3 وَمِنَ النَّاسِ مَنْ يَقُولُ ءَامَنَّا بِاللَّهِ وَبِالْيَوْمِ الْأَخِرِ
and they are not believers. 2: 8	4 ■ وَمَا هُمْ بِمُؤْمِنِينَ
And (all) honour belongs to God and to His messenger and to the believers. 63: 8	5 وَلِلَّهِ الْعِزَّةُ وَلِرَسُولِهِ وَلِلْمُؤْمِنِينَ
From the Sacred Mosque to the Farther Mosque. 17: 1	6 مِنَ الْمَسْجِدِ الْحَرَامِ إِلَى الْمَسْجِدِ الْأَقْصَى
With a vessel (made) from silver. 76: 15	7 بِءَانِيَةٍ مِنْ فِضَّةٍ
From before the Prayer of dawn. 24: 58	8 مِنْ قَبْلِ صَلٰوةِ الْفَجْرِ
and from after the Prayer of 'Isha'. 24: 58	9 وَمِنْ بَعْدِ صَلٰوةِ الْعِشَاءِ
Your possessions and your children are only a test. 64: 15	10 إِنَّمَا أَمْوَالُكُمْ وَأَوْلَادُكُمْ فِتْنَةٌ
And God - with Him - is a great reward. 64: 15	11 وَاللَّهُ عِنْدَهُ أَجْرٌ عَظِيمٌ
At the Sacred Mosque (in Makkah). 2: 191	12 عِنْدَ الْمَسْجِدِ الْحَرَامِ
Indeed the religion with God is Islam. 3: 19	13 إِنَّ الدِّينَ عِنْدَ اللَّهِ الْإِسْلَامُ
Indeed, God is with the steadfast ones. 2: 153	14 إِنَّ اللَّهَ مَعَ الصَّابِرِينَ
Peace (be) on you! 39: 73	15 سَلَامٌ عَلَيْكُمْ

Notes for text above

■ *Line 1:* The preposition مِنَ has a fat-hah on the نَ instead of a sukun for linking it to the following word.

The word اللَّهِ is genitive because it is controlled by the preposition بِ .

■ *Line 2:* The word اللَّهِ is genitive because it indicates possession.

■ *Line 4:* The sentence is a negative sentence beginning with مَا . Now notice the بِ attached to مُؤْمِنِينَ . In negative sentences beginning with مَا (not) or لَسْتُ (I am not), لَسْتَ (you are not), لَيْسَ (he is not), the following noun is often prefixed by the preposition بِ which is not translated: e.g.

مَا هُوَ بِشَاعِرٍ   He is not a poet.

أَلَسْتُ بِرَبِّكُمْ   Am I not your Lord?

Unit 9

إنَّ and

"her sisters"

In previous Units, we have come across the particle إِنَّ in some phrases and sentences. We have also learnt that the noun controlled by إِنَّ is in the accusative. Here we want to give some more examples of the use of إِنَّ .

In Arabic, a simple sentence which does not have a verb and which begins with a noun is called **a nominal sentence**.

إِنَّ اللَّهَ غَفُورٌ رَحِيمٌ

In the above sentence, the word اللَّهَ is called the 'noun of إِنَّ '. It is singular and ends with a fat-hah. The noun of إِنَّ is always in the accusative.

> A **predicate** gives information about the first part of a sentence. The word for predicate in Arabic is **khabar** which means **information**.

The word غَفُورٌ is called 'the predicate of إِنَّ '. It is singular and ends with dammah. The word for predicate in Arabic is خَبَر and means 'information'. The predicate gives information about the noun of إِنَّ . The predicate of إِنَّ - if it is a noun or adjective - is in the nominative.

Some more examples - **read from right to left**:

Predicate of إِنَّ	Noun of إِنَّ	
عَلِيمٌ حَكِيمٌ	اللَّهَ إِنَّ	Indeed God is Knowing, Wise.
وَاسِعَةٌ	أَرْضَ اللَّهِ إِنَّ	Indeed God's earth is spacious.
لَكَاذِبُونَ	الْمُنَافِقِينَ إِنَّ	Indeed the hypocrites are liars.

Consider Time

The word الْعَصْر has the sense of time through the ages. It also means afternoon. There are many words in the Qur'an for time. وَقْت - the time of day; يَوْم - a day or an aeon in time; دَهْر - time in eternity; حِين - a period of time; سَاعَة - a moment.

The verses in line 2 are the first of Suratu-l 'Asr. This short surah deals with the real purpose of the human being on earth - to believe in God and do good deeds. It also stresses the believers' need for mutual support and solidarity. The surah summarizes the Qur'anic view of history and human worth and success. It was a habit of some Companions of the Prophet to recite Suratu-l 'Asr at the end of their meetings.

There are other particles, known in Arabic grammar as 'the sisters of إِنَّ ' which have the same effect as إِنَّ . The frequently used ones in the Qur'an are:

أَنَّ that; كَأَنَّ as if; لٰكِنَّ but; لَعَلَّ perhaps

Predicate	Noun	
بِيَدِ اللَّهِ	الْفَضْلَ وَأَنَّ	And that (all) grace is in God's hand.
قَرِيبٌ	السَّاعَةَ وَلَعَلَّ	And perhaps the Hour is near.
لَا يَعْلَمُونَ	أَكْثَرَ النَّاسِ وَلٰكِنَّ	But most people do not know.
لَا يَفْقَهُونَ	الْمُنَافِقِينَ وَلٰكِنَّ	But the hypocrites do not understand.

إِنَّ and 'her sisters' are often used with attached pronouns. The following combinations occur in the Qur'an:

إِنَّ - إِنَّهُ إِنَّهَا إِنَّكَ إِنَّكُمْ

أَنَّ - أَنَّهُ أَنَّهَا أَنَّكَ أَنَّكُمْ

لٰكِنَّ - لٰكِنَّهُ لٰكِنِّي لٰكِنَّهُمْ لٰكِنَّكُمْ

لَعَلَّ - لَعَلَّهُ لَعَلِّي لَعَلَّكُمْ لَعَلَّهُمْ لَعَلَّنَا

1	Indeed the earth belongs to God. 7: 128	إِنَّ ٱلْأَرْضَ لِلَّهِ
2	By Time! Surely the human being is in loss. 103: 1-2	وَٱلْعَصْرِ إِنَّ ٱلْإِنْسَانَ لَفِى خُسْرٍ
3	Truly, the mercy of God is near. 7: 56	إِنَّ رَحْمَةَ ٱللَّهِ قَرِيبٌ
4	Indeed, in that is a sign for the believers. 15: 77	إِنَّ فِى ذٰلِكَ لَأَيَةً لِّلْمُؤْمِنِينَ
5	Indeed the righteous shall be in bliss and the corrupt shall be in hell. 82:13-14	إِنَّ ٱلْأَبْرَارَ لَفِى نَعِيمٍ وَإِنَّ ٱلْفُجَّارَ لَفِى جَحِيمٍ
6	The hypocrites are indeed liars. 63: 1	إِنَّ ٱلْمُنَافِقِينَ لَكَاذِبُونَ
7	The righteous shall be in gardens and in bliss. 10: 45 and 52: 17	إِنَّ ٱلْمُتَّقِينَ فِى جَنَّاتٍ وَنَعِيمٍ
8 ■	And know that among you (is) the messenger of God. 49: 7	وَٱعْلَمُوا أَنَّ فِيكُمْ رَسُولَ ٱللَّهِ
9	And that (all) bounty is in God's hand. 57: 29	وَأَنَّ ٱلْفَضْلَ بِيَدِ ٱللَّهِ
10 ■	But the hypocrites do not understand. 63: 7	وَلَٰكِنَّ ٱلْمُنَافِقِينَ لَا يَفْقَهُونَ
11 ■	It is the truth from your Lord, but most people do not believe. 11: 17	إِنَّهُ ٱلْحَقُّ مِنْ رَبِّكَ وَلَٰكِنَّ أَكْثَرَ ٱلنَّاسِ لَا يُؤْمِنُونَ
12	Perhaps the Hour is near. 42: 17	لَعَلَّ ٱلسَّاعَةَ قَرِيبٌ
13	And God over everything is Powerful. 2: 254	وَٱللَّهُ عَلَىٰ كُلِّ شَىْءٍ قَدِيرٌ
14	Indeed, God over everything is Powerful. 2: 20	إِنَّ ٱللَّهَ عَلَىٰ كُلِّ شَىْءٍ قَدِيرٌ
15 ■	But God is the Possessor of grace for all the worlds. 2: 251	وَلَٰكِنَّ ٱللَّهَ ذُو فَضْلٍ عَلَى ٱلْعَٰلَمِينَ

Notes for text above

■ **Line 8:** The word اعْلَمُوا - Know! - is a verb and is imperative plural.

■ **Line 10:** The words لَا يَفْقَهُونَ mean 'they do not understand'.

■ **Line 11:** لَا يُؤْمِنُونَ means 'they do not believe'.

■ **Line 15:** The word ذُو means 'possessor of'. It is masculine and nominative. The word which comes after it is in the genitive.

عَصْر	time; mid-afternoon
خُسْر	loss
قَرِيب	near
فَاجِر / فُجَّار	corrupt/pl.
فَقِهَ / يَفْقَهُ	to understand

Unit 10

Possession - the Idafah construction

In a previous Unit, we have mentioned briefly phrases like كِتَابُ اللَّهِ , **the** book **of** Allah.

The phrase is made up of two nouns which are closely linked and cannot usually be separated.

In the phrase كِتَابُ اللَّهِ , the first noun كِتَابُ is called the مُضَاف and means 'the book'. The mudaf (meaning 'linked') is always <u>definite</u> even though it does not have the definite article .

The second noun اللَّهِ is called the مُضَاف إلَيْهِ which means 'linked to it'. It shows the possessor and in this example means '**of** Allah'. The mudaf ilayhi is always in the genitive. Below are some examples of the idafah construction. **Read from right to left.**

		mudaf ilayhi	mudaf
1	the night of Power	الْقَدْرِ	لَيْلَةُ
2	with the Sustainer of mankind	النَّاسِ	بِرَبِّ
3	(from) the evil of an envious one	حَاسِدٍ	(مِنْ) شَرِّ
4	the Lord of the two easts	الْمَشْرِقَيْنِ	رَبُّ
5	the Sustainer of the worlds	الْعَالَمِينَ	رَبُّ
6	the Sustainer of the heavens	السَّمَاوَاتِ	رَبُّ
7	two messengers of your Lord	رَبِّكَ	رَسُولَا
8	the wrongdoers of themselves	أَنْفُسِهِمْ	ظَالِمِي

Nouns in the dual and masculine sound plural lose their final ن when they are mudaf.

In example 7 above, the dual رَسُولَانِ has lost its نِ .

In example 8 above, the plural ظَالِمِينَ has lost its نَ .

Normally no word must come between the 'Mudaf' and the 'Mudaf ilayhi'.

However, notice in line 10 opposite, the word هَـٰذَا this, comes between the mudaf رَبَّ and the mudaf ilayhi الْبَيْتِ . Demonstratives like هَـٰذَا and هَـٰذِهِ are the only words which can come between the two nouns in an idafah construction.

A word with an attached pronoun is considered to be a mudaf and so is definite. An adjective describing such a word will therefore have the definite article. e.g. عِنْدَ بَيْتِكَ الْمُكَرَّمِ - *near* Your sanctified house.

The word بَيْت is definite because it is a mudaf. Its adjective مُكَرَّم must also be definite and so has ال . See line 15 opposite for another example.

Awesome vastness

الْعَالَمِين is the sound masculine plural of الْعَالَم - the world or the universe. Every created species is an 'alam or a world. The Qur'an speaks of worlds or 'universes' in the plural - thus pointing to the unimaginable and awesome vastness of God's creation.

لَيْلَةُ الْقَدْرِ

The Night of Power or Destiny is the night in which the Qur'an was first revealed to the Prophet Muhammad, peace be on him, as 'guidance for mankind'. It is in the blessed month of Ramadan.

أَعُوذُ	I seek refuge
وَسْوَسَ / يُوَسْوِسُ	to whisper
وَسْوَاس	whisperer
صَدْرٌ / صُدُورٌ	heart, chest/pl.
أَلْف	a thousand

In the name of Allah, most Gracious, most Merciful. 1: 1	١ ● بِسْمِ اللَّهِ الرَّحْمَـٰنِ الرَّحِيمِ
All praise is for Allah, the Sustainer of the worlds, the most Gracious, the most Merciful 1: 2-3	٢ اَلْحَمْدُ لِلَّهِ رَبِّ الْعَـٰلَمِينَ الرَّحْمَـٰنِ الرَّحِيمِ
Ruler of the day of Judgment. 1: 4	٣ مَـٰلِكِ يَوْمِ الدِّينِ
Say: I seek protection with the Sustainer of mankind, the Sovereign of mankind 114: 1-2	٤ ● قُلْ أَعُوذُ بِرَبِّ النَّاسِ مَلِكِ النَّاسِ
the God of mankind, from the evil of the elusive whisperer 114: 3-4	٥ إِلَـٰهِ النَّاسِ مِنْ شَرِّ الْوَسْوَاسِ الْخَنَّاسِ
who whispers into the hearts of people 114: 5	٦ الَّذِى يُوَسْوِسُ فِى صُدُورِ النَّاسِ
from among the jinn and mankind. 114: 6	٧ ● مِنَ الْجِنَّةِ وَالنَّاسِ
When God's help comes. 110: 1	٨ إِذَا جَاءَ نَصْرُ اللَّهِ
For the security of the Quraysh, their security during the journey of winter and of summer ... 106: 1-2	٩ ● لِإِيلَافِ قُرَيْشٍ إِيلَافِهِمْ رِحْلَةَ الشِّتَاءِ وَالصَّيْفِ
let them therefore worship the Lord of this house. 106: 3	١٠ فَلْيَعْبُدُوا رَبَّ هَـٰذَا الْبَيْتِ
The Night of Power is better than a thousand months. 97: 3	١١ لَيْلَةُ الْقَدْرِ خَيْرٌ مِنْ أَلْفِ شَهْرٍ
The Lord of the two easts and the Lord of the two wests. 55: 17	١٢ رَبُّ الْمَشْرِقَيْنِ وَرَبُّ الْمَغْرِبَيْنِ
We are indeed both messengers of your Lord. 20: 47	١٣ إِنَّا رَسُولَا رَبِّكَ
The Lord of the heavens and of the earth and of what is between them both. 78: 37	١٤ رَبُّ السَّمَـٰوَٰتِ وَالْأَرْضِ وَمَا بَيْنَهُمَا
Your Lord and the Lord of your early ancestors. 26: 26	١٥ ● رَبُّكُمْ وَرَبُّ ءَابَاءِكُمُ الْأَوَّلِينَ

Notes for text above

● *Line 2:* The word لِلَّهِ ends with a kasrah and is genitive because it is controlled by the preposition لِ . The words الرَّحِيمِ , الرَّحْمَـٰنِ and مَـٰلِكِ are all in the genitive in apposition to or agreeing with لِلَّهِ .

● *Line 4:* The word رَبِّ is in the genitive because it is controlled by the preposition بِ . The following words مَـٰلِكِ and إِلَـٰهِ are in the genitive because they are in apposition to رَبِّ . The word النَّاسِ in

lines 4, 5 and 6 are all in the genitive because they are mudaf ilayhi.

● *Line 7:* The word النَّاسِ is genitive because it is controlled by the preposition مِنْ , *from.*

● *Line 9:* رِحْلَةَ is accusative and is used as an adverb: '**during** *the journey*'.

● *Line 15:* The adjective اَلْأَوَّلِينَ is genitive to agree with its noun ءَابَاءِ which is the mudaf ilayhi of رَبُّ .

The **root letters** of an Arabic word are sometimes called **radicals**.

The root word is sometimes referred to simply as **the root**.

Most Arabic words have three main letters. These are called **root letters**. The simplest word from these three root letters has the meaning of **he + the past tense.**

The word خَلَقَ means 'He created.'

The root letters in خَلَقَ are خ ل ق . خَلَقَ is a **root word**. It only has root letters.

New words grow like a tree from the root words. Letters are added to the root and vowels and signs are added or changed to form new words.

Letters may be added:

i.   before the first root letter, as in: يَخْلُقُ

ii.   between the root letters   خَالِق

iii   after the last root letter   خَلَقُوا

iv.   by doubling letters (using a shaddah)   خَلَّاق

v.   by a combination of the above.   إِخْتِلَاق

Letters used for adding to the root word are:

أ ا ت ة س ل م ن هـ و ي

These letters, apart from the ta' marbutah ة , are contained in the word

سَأَلْتُمُونِيهَا which means 'You asked me about them'. Soon we hope you will

understand how one word in Arabic can mean so much.

Words are formed from the root word according to a variety of word patterns. You can often tell the meaning of a word from the word pattern. We will see how this happens as we go along. But let us go back to خَلَقَ .

خَلَقَ means 'He created.'

The pronoun 'He' is built into the form of the verb خَلَقَ . So usually there is no need for a separate word for 'He'.

Arabic is a language of patterns and if you can match one pattern to another, you can get some idea of the meaning of a word. Other verbs with different root letters but which have the same pattern as خَلَقَ may also mean 'He + the past tense'. Therefore:

جَعَلَ   He made.   دَخَلَ   He entered.   خَرَجَ   He went out.

The middle root letter in خَلَقَ has a fat-hah.

In some root words, the middle root letter has a kasrah, for example:

عَمِلَ   He worked.   عَلِمَ   He knew.   سَمِعَ   He heard.

In a few cases, the middle root letter has a dammah, for example:

كَبُرَ   It was great   كَثُرَ   It was plentiful

Precision

بَدَأَ – بَرَأَ – خَلَقَ

فَطَرَ – جَعَلَ

There are a few words in the Qur'an meaning 'to make' or 'to create'. Each has a precise meaning which is often not conveyed in English translations.

bada'a - means to begin or originate;

bara'a - means to bring into existence from nothing;

khalaqa - has the sense of to bring into existence for the first time and define the nature and disposition of what is created.

fatara - means to originate. It has the basic meaning of to break or to split.

ja'ala - has the sense of to make and has a wide variety of meanings including to appoint or to change something.

The following words

بَرَأَ – خَلَقَ – فَطَرَ

are used only for Allah.

Read the following from right to left, starting from the root words in Arabic.
In the column 'Words from Root Words', note the letters which are added to the root words.

Added Letters	Words formed from Roots Words	Root Words
م و	eaten مَأْكُول	أَكَلَ he ate
ت و ن	you (pl.) command تَأْمُرُونَ	أَمَرَ he commanded
ة	congregation جُمُعَة	جَمَعَ he gathered
و	leaving, exit خُرُوج	خَرَجَ he went out
ا	Creator خَالِق	خَلَقَ He created
ي و ن	they (pl.) enter يَدْخُلُونَ	دَخَلَ he entered
م	place of prostration مَسْجِد	سَجَدَ he prostrated
doubled ل	he taught عَلَّمَ	عَلِمَ he knew
ي س ت و ن	They ask forgiveness of Him يَسْتَغْفِرُونَهُ	غَفَرَ he forgave
م س ت + ي	straight مُسْتَقِيم	قَامَ he stood
ا	book, scripture كِتَاب	كَتَبَ he wrote
ف ا	disbelievers كُفَّار	كَفَرَ he disbelieved
م	place مَكَان	كَانَ he was
و ا turned to	death مَوْت	مَاتَ he died
أ ا	helpers أَنْصَار	نَصَرَ he helped

Note: The alif in مَاتَ is turned into a و in مَوْت
The alif in قَام is turned into a ي in مستقيم

Unit 12

Sentences begining with a root word

> A **verb** is the doing or the action word in a sentence.
>
> The **tense** of a verb refers to the time of an action.

Each sentence on the opposite page begins with a verb in the past tense. (Tense refers to the time of an action.) Each verb has only the three root letters and therefore means 'He + the past tense'.

Notice again that all the verbs come first in these sentences and that the word 'He' is built into each verb.

Sentences

A sentence is a word or group of words which makes complete sense.

In Section One, we read sentences in Arabic without verbs which made complete sense.

We learnt that sentences beginning with a noun are called **'nominal sentences'**.

Verbal Sentences

It is common in Arabic for sentences to begin with a verb. Sentences which begin with a verb are called 'verbal sentences'. An example of such a sentence is:

خَـلَقَ اللَّهُ الأَرْضَ   God created the earth.

In the above sentence, the verb is   خَـلَقَ .

The **subject** of a sentence is the part which says who or what you are talking about. You can know the subject of a sentence by asking the question 'who?' or 'what?' **before** the verb. If you ask, 'who created?' the answer - 'God' - is the subject of the sentence.

The subject of a sentence in Arabic is in the **nominative** case. The word اللَّهُ in the above sentence is therefore nominative. It is also singular and so ends with a dammah.

A **'direct object'** of a sentence is the person or thing which is directly affected by the verb. In the above sentence the object is 'the earth'. (You know the direct object by asking the question 'what?' or 'whom?' **after** the verb. If you ask, 'created what?' the answer - 'the earth' - is the object of the sentence.)

In Arabic, the object of a sentence is in the **accusative**. الأَرْضَ is therefore accusative and ends with a fat-hah.

Word order

In Arabic, when the subject of the verb is specified, like اللَّهُ in the sentence above, the verb normally comes first, followed by the subject and then the rest of the sentence.

We can see this in sentence 8 opposite. The subject of the sentence 'Musa' follows the verb.

Be prepared for quite a different word order in Arabic phrases and sentences from what you are used to in English.

In the English translation opposite, words between brackets are added to complete the meaning of a sentence. There is no corresponding Arabic for the words in brackets.

Note on line 10 opposite: الطَّاغُوت

There is no single word for Taghut in English. Taghut may refer to idols or any false objects of worship, or any evil practices which take a person away from the straight path of obedience to God. It may also refer to tyrannical rulers or systems.

رَبّ

There is no single word in English for Rabb. Rabb means 'one who owns something and looks after it well'. We may translate it as 'Cherisher and Sustainer' when it refers to God. Often only the word 'Lord' or the word 'Sustainer' is used for Rabb, but we should always bear in mind its wider meaning.

English	Arabic	#
He gathered wealth. 104: 2	جَمَعَ مَالاً	1
He created the earth. 20: 4	خَلَقَ الْأَرْضَ	2
He entered the city. 28:15	دَخَلَ الْمَدِينَةَ	3
He went out from it (the city). 28: 21	خَرَجَ مِنْهَا	4
He called (upon) his Sustainer. 39: 8	دَعَا رَبَّهُ	■ 5
So he called (upon) his Sustainer. 44: 22	فَدَعَا رَبَّهُ	■ 6
And he remembered God much. 33: 21	وَذَكَرَ اللَّهَ كَثِيراً	7
So Musa returned to his people. 7: 150	فَرَجَعَ مُوسَى إِلَى قَوْمِهِ	■ 8
He did righteous work. 18: 88	عَمِلَ عَمَلاً صَالِحاً	9
He has worshipped false gods. 5: 60	عَبَدَ الطَّاغُوتَ	10
So He forgave him. 28:16	فَغَفَرَ لَهُ	11
Who has done this with our gods? 21:59	مَنْ فَعَلَ هَـٰذَا بِآلِهَتِنَا	■ 12
He said: I (am) better than he. 38: 76	قَالَ أَنَا خَيْرٌ مِنْهُ	■ 13
He found beside her sustenance. 3: 37	وَجَدَ عِنْدَهَا رِزْقاً	14
This (is) what the Beneficent has promised. 36: 52	هَـٰذَا مَا وَعَدَ الرَّحْمَـٰنُ	■ 15

Glossary:

مَالٌ wealth

مَدِينَةٌ city

طَاغُوت false gods

رَجَعَ to return

Notes for text above

■ *Line 5:* The verb دَعَا is known as a weak verb. The alif in دَعَا stands for the letter و . The root letters of دَعَا are د ع و .

■ *Lines 6 & 8:* The letter ف *and, and so,* is always attached to the following word.

The word مُوسَى does not change. It has the same form for all cases.

■ *Line 12:* The word بِآلِهَتِنَا = بِ + آلِهَةِ + نَا

- 'with our gods'.

■ *Line 13:* The verb قَالَ 'he said' is known as a hollow verb. It is like the verb كَانَ , 'he was'.

The root letters of قَالَ are ق و ل .

The root letters of كَانَ are ك و ن .

■ *Line 15:* The particle مَا means '*what*'. Note that مَا can also mean '*not*', negating the verb in the past tense.

Tense refers to the time of an action.
The term Past Tense is used to refer to the Arabic *Madi*.
In many grammar books, Madi is also referred to as the Perfect Tense since it refers to actions which are 'perfect' or complete.
It is important to remember that the Madi in Arabic does not always refer to actions in the past. It may be used for making a wish or in 'conditional sentences' (see Unit 40).
The actual tense of a verb must be determined by its context.

The verb كَتَبَ is a root word. It is a verb in the past tense. It means '**He wrote**'.

The word '**He**' is built into the word كَتَبَ .

If you add the letter ت with a sukun to the root word, you form the new word كَتَبَتْ . The suffix ت with a sukun tells you that كَتَبَتْ means '**She** wrote'.
A letter or letters added **after** a word is called a **suffix**.

Verbs having the suffix ت will mean 'she + the past tense'. Thus:

سَمِعَ	he heard	عَلِمَ	he knew
سَمِعَتْ	heard	عَلِمَتْ	she knew

From كَتَبَ we also get other words by adding different suffixes:

كَتَبْتَ you (m.s.) wrote, كَتَبْتِ you (f.s.) wrote, كَتَبْتُ I wrote.
(Abbreviations: m.s. = masculine singular; f.s. = feminine singular)

In the three words above, notice that a sukun is placed on the last root letter.
The suffix or added ending in all the above words is the letter ت . But each ت has a different vowel.

In the word كَتَبْتَ, the last ت with the fat-hah stands for 'you' masculine singular (m.s.).

In the word كَتَبْتِ, the last ت with the kasrah stands for 'you' feminine singular (f.s.).

In the word كَتَبْتُ, the last ت with the dammah stands for 'I' .

Other singular verbs in the past tense will have the same endings. Thus:

A car – سَيَّارَةٌ

In modern Arabic, sayyarah is a car. In Surah Yusuf, *sayyarah* refers to the caravan or the company of travellers that found Yusuf in a well after he had been taken away and abandoned there by his jealous brothers. They went back to their father and said that a wolf had eaten Yusuf, a story which the father, Prophet Ya'qub - peace be on him, did not believe. The caravan travelled on to Egypt and sold Yusuf to the ruler of Egypt in whose household he grew up. The amazing story of Yusuf is told at some length in the Qur'an.

The word sayyarah comes from the verb *sara* which means to go, to move or to travel.

you (m.s.) went out	خَرَجْتَ	دَخَلْتَ	you (m.s.) entered
you (f.s.) went out	خَرَجْتِ	دَخَلْتِ	You (f.s.) entered
I went out	خَرَجْتُ	دَخَلْتُ	I entered

Below is a chart with the singular forms of two verbs in the past tense. **Read from the right and then down.**

	Singular		Singular		
he did	فَعَلَ	كَتَبَ	he wrote	3.m.
she did	فَعَلَتْ	كَتَبَتْ	she wrote	3.f.
you did	فَعَلْتَ	كَتَبْتَ	you wrote	2.m.
you did	فَعَلْتِ	كَتَبْتِ	you wrote	2.f.
I did	فَعَلْتُ	كَتَبْتُ	I wrote	1.m. & f.

God has heard. 58: 1	1	سَمِعَ اللّهُ
So when she heard about their gossip. 12: 31	2	فَلَمَّا سَمِعَتْ بِمَكْرِهِنَّ
She bore a burden. 7: 189	3	حَمَلَتْ حَمْلاً
So she watched over him from afar. 28: 11	4	فَبَصُرَتْ بِهِ عَن جُنُبٍ
And a caravan came. 12: 19	5	وَجَاءَتْ سَيَّارَةٌ
And indeed Our messengers came (to) Ibrahim with the good news. 11: 69	6	وَلَقَدْ جَاءَتْ رُسُلُنَا إِبْرَاهِيمَ بِالْبُشْرَى
You created me from fire... 7: 12	7	خَلَقْتَنِي مِن نَّارٍ
and You created him from clay. 7: 12	8	وَخَلَقْتَهُ مِن طِينٍ
Have you seen the one who has rejected/disbelieved in Our signs? 19: 77	9	أَرَأَيْتَ الَّذِي كَفَرَ بِآيَاتِنَا
And you killed someone. 20: 40	10	وَقَتَلْتَ نَفْساً
They said: O Maryam! Indeed you have come (with) an amazing thing. 19: 27	11	قَالُوا يَا مَرْيَمُ لَقَدْ جِئْتِ شَيْئًا فَرِيًّا
He said: My Lord! Indeed I have killed someone from among them. 28: 33	12	قَالَ رَبِّ إِنِّي قَتَلْتُ مِنْهُمْ نَفْساً
And I made for him wealth extensive. 74: 12	13	وَجَعَلْتُ لَهُ مَالاً مَّمْدُودًا
I saw eleven planets and the sun and the moon... 12: 4	14	رَأَيْتُ أَحَدَ عَشَرَ كَوْكَبًا وَالشَّمْسَ وَالْقَمَرَ
I have not created jinn and mankind except that they may worship me. 51: 56	15	مَا خَلَقْتُ الْجِنَّ وَالْإِنسَ إِلاَّ لِيَعْبُدُونِ

Notes for text above

■ **Line 6:** The word رُسُلُ *messengers*, is a broken plural of رَسُولُ and is here considered to be feminine singular. The verb جَاءَتْ is therefore feminine singular. • The word الْبُشْرَى means 'the good news'.

■ **Line 9:** The particle أ introduces a question.

• بِآيَاتِنَا = بِ + ءَايَاتِ + نَا - *in Our signs*

■ **Line 11:** يَا + مَرْيَمُ = يَا مَرْيَمُ - *O Maryam!*

■ **Line 12:** The preposition مِن is translated as 'from among'.

■ **Line 15:** لِيَعْبُدُونِ = لِ + يَعْبُدُو + ن - *so that + they may worship + me.* The نِ is short for نِي.

فَرِيًّا	amazing	مَكْرِ	plot, gossip
أَحَدَ عَشَرَ	eleven	طِينٍ	clay
كَوْكَبٌ	planet	الَّذِي	the one who

Unit 14

The verb: past tense, singular, dual & plural

To **conjugate** a verb is to show its various forms for the singular, dual and plural - masculine and feminine, in a particular tense.

Below is a chart with the complete conjugation of the verb كَتَبَ in the past tense. To conjugate a verb is to show its various forms.

In the past tense, all changes to the verb are made by adding suffixes to the root word.

The suffixes tell who did the action. For example, the suffix تُ indicates 'I' and the suffix نَا indicates '**We**'.

You may use the chart below as a reference. You are not expected at this stage to remember all the endings of the verb in the past tense before going on. However, the sooner you know them the better.

Plural		Dual		Singular		
they wrote	كَتَبُوا	they wrote	كَتَبَا	he wrote	كَتَبَ	3.m.
they wrote	كَتَبْنَ	they wrote	كَتَبَتَا	she wrote	كَتَبَتْ	3.f.
you wrote	كَتَبْتُم	you wrote	كَتَبْتُمَا	you wrote	كَتَبْتَ	2.m.
you wrote	كَتَبْتُنَّ	you wrote	كَتَبْتُمَا	you wrote	كَتَبْتِ	2.f.
we wrote	كَتَبْنَا	we wrote	كَتَبْنَا	I wrote	كَتَبْتُ	1.m & f.

From the above chart, you will see that verbs are classified according to:

i. **Number** - singular, dual or plural
ii. **Gender** - masculine or feminine
iii. **Person** - 3rd, 2nd or 1st person.

(They are also classified according to **tense** (e.g. past or present), **voice** (active or passive) and **mood** - but we will explain what these mean later.)

Number

We already know from Section One, that words in Arabic can be singular, dual or plural. Singular refers to one, dual refers to two, and plural refers to more than two. This applies to verbs as well.

In the last Unit, we dealt with the singular forms of the verb in the past tense. The dual forms do not occur very frequently. The verbs in lines 2 and 5 opposite are dual.

In the plural of the past tense, notice that there is an alif written, but not pronounced, at the end of the masculine, 3rd person form: كَتَبُوا *they wrote*. In the Madinah Mus-haf, a small circle is placed above this alif to show that it is not pronounced.

Notice the difference in pronunciation and meaning between كَتَبْنَ *they (f) wrote*, and كَتَبْنَا *we wrote*.

Hint: The verbs in the second person past tense all have the same endings as their respective separate pronouns.. Repeating each verb with its pronoun may help in memorizing, e.g. أَنْتَ كَتَبْتَ   أَنْتِ كَتَبْتِ   أَنْتُم كَتَبْتُم

Faith and good works

Faith and good works are frequently mentioned together in the Qur'an. It is not sufficient to believe in God. Belief has to be supported and confirmed by righteous action. Noone lives in a vacuum. Either one does good deeds, or remains idle and lazy, or does wrong and evil deeds.

The words

ءَامَنُوا وَ عَمِلُوا الصَّالِحَات

- those who 'have believed and done good works' (lines 11 & 12 opposite) occur more than fifty times together in the Qur'an.

English	Arabic	#
He made darkness and light. 6: 1	جَعَلَ الظُّلُمَـٰتِ وَالنُّورَ	1
They both made partners unto Him. 7: 190	جَعَلَا لَهُ شُرَكَاءَ	2
And they made partners unto God. 13: 33	وَجَعَلُوا لِلَّهِ شُرَكَاءَ	3
And He found you wandering and guided (you). 93: 7	وَوَجَدَكَ ضَآلًّا فَهَدَى	4
And they (both) found one of Our servants (lit. a servant from Our servants). 88: 65	وَوَجَدَا عَبْدًا مِنْ عِبَادِنَا	5
They found their merchandise. 12: 65	وَجَدُوا بِضَاعَتَهُمْ	6
The messenger has believed. 2: 285	ءَامَنَ الرَّسُولُ	7 ■
Surely, I believed in your Lord. 36: 25	إِنِّى ءَامَنتُ بِرَبِّكُمْ	8
Our Sustainer! We have believed... 5: 83	رَبَّنَا ءَامَنَّا	9 ■
What have they created of the earth? 35: 40	مَاذَا خَلَقُوا مِنَ الْأَرْضِ	10 ■
And those who have believed...	وَالَّذِينَ ءَامَنُوا	11 ■
...and have done good works...	وَعَمِلُوا الصَّـٰلِحَاتِ	12
...those are the companions of Paradise. 2: 82	أُوْلَـٰئِكَ أَصْحَابُ الْجَنَّةِ	13
And those who have disbelieved and denied Our signs...	وَالَّذِينَ كَفَرُوا وَكَذَّبُوا بِـَٔايَاتِنَا	14 ■
...those are the companions of the Fire. 2: 39	أُوْلَـٰئِكَ أَصْحَابُ النَّارِ	15

Notes for text above

■ *Line 7:* The verb ءَامَنَ in line 7 is a Form IV verb; other past tense forms of this verb occur in lines 8, 9 and 11.

■ *Line 9:* The word رَبَّ is accusative. In addressing someone, the accusative is used:

(i) when the word has an attached pronoun as in رَبَّنَا , *Our Sustainer!*

(ii) when it is followed by a word in the genitive, e.g.

يَا مَعْشَرَ الْجِنِّ وَالْإِنسِ - *O company of jinn and mankind!*

Otherwise, the nominative is used: a single dammah for words in the singular e.g.

يَا مُحَمَّدُ , *O Muhammad!*

■ *Line 10:* The preposition مِنْ is translated as 'of'.

■ *Lines 11 & 14:* الَّذِينَ *those who*, is the masculine plural of الَّذِى , *the one who.*

اللَّه

The word 'Allah' is grammatically masculine singular but it has no gender connotations. Also, the word Allah does not have any plural form - unlike the word 'god' in English or 'ilah' in Arabic.

Number (continued)

Feminine plural past tense verbs end with ـنَ which is a short vowel. For example:

دَخَلْنَ they (f) entered   كَتَبْنَ they (f) wrote.

However, first person plural verbs end with نَا which is a long vowel:

دَخَلْنَا we entered   كَتَبْنَا we wrote.

Be careful when reading to keep short vowels short and lengthen the long vowels. Meanings change when you lengthen vowels. You can see that the endings of words are very important in Arabic.

Gender

Verbs, like pronouns, in Arabic may be either masculine (m.) or feminine (f.). There is no neuter gender. Study the following:

جَاءَ He has come   جَاءَ It has come.

جَاءَ رَجُلٌ A man came   جَاءَ الْحَقُّ The Truth has come.

جَاءَتْ She came   جَاءَتْ سَيَّارَةٌ A caravan came.

A masculine singular noun takes a verb in the masculine. The noun الْحَقُّ is masculine and the verb جَاءَ is also masculine.

A feminine singular noun takes a verb in the feminine. The noun سَيَّارَةٌ is feminine because it ends with ta' marbutah ة . Its verb جَاءَتْ is also feminine - it ends with تْ

More on the agreement of subjects and verbs

i. When a verb comes first in a sentence and its subject is 3rd person, it is always singular - even if the subject is singular, dual or plural. (See lines 12 - 15.)

ii. When a verb comes first in a sentence, it can be masculine even if the subject is grammatically feminine. e.g. in line 14, the subject الْمُؤْمِنَاتُ is feminine plural but its verb جَاءَ is masculine singular.

iii. The verb occurring first in a sentence is singular even if the subject is plural. But a following verb with the same plural subject will be plural. In line 15, the first verb جَاءَ is singular but the second verb دَخَلُوا is plural. The subject of both verbs is إِخْوَةٌ , *the brothers.*

الْمَاء

The verse in line 4 opposite, expresses a profound truth: that water is necessary for the emergence and development of life. Life depends on water. Read this verse with the previous amazing verse of the Qur'an, 21: 29.

Hint on translating into English:

First identify the subject of the Arabic sentence. If the subject is a noun, it must be in the nominative case. For example, in line 13 opposite, the subject must be رُسُلُنَا which is nominative. In line 14, the subject of the verb جَاءَ is الْمُؤْمِنَاتُ which is nominative.

ميثَاقٌ   pledge, covenant

غَلِيظٌ   solemn, strong

طَهُورٌ   pure

بَيِّنَاتٌ   clear teachings

They (f.) took from you a solemn pledge. 4: 21	1 أَخَذْنَ مِنكُم مِّيثَاقًا غَلِيظًا
So when they (f.) saw him... 12: 31	2 فَلَمَّا رَأَيْنَهُ
We created the heavens and the earth. 50: 16	3 ■ خَلَقْنَا السَّمَـٰوَٰتِ وَالْأَرْضَ
And We made from water every living thing. 21: 30	4 ■ وَجَعَلْنَا مِنَ الْمَاءِ كُلَّ شَيْءٍ حَيٍّ
We sent down from the sky pure water. 25: 48	5 ■ أَنزَلْنَا مِنَ السَّمَاءِ مَاءً طَهُورًا
We have heard and we have obeyed. 2: 285	6 سَمِعْنَا وَأَطَعْنَا
Indeed We did send our messengers with clear teachings. 57: 25	7 ■ لَقَدْ أَرْسَلْنَا رُسُلَنَا بِالْبَيِّنَاتِ
And indeed We did send Musa with our signs. 11: 96	8 ■ وَلَقَدْ أَرْسَلْنَا مُوسَى بِـَٔايَاتِنَا
A man came. 28: 20	9 جَاءَ رَجُلٌ
The Truth has come. 17: 81	10 جَاءَ الْحَقُّ
A caravan came. 12: 19	11 جَاءَتْ سَيَّارَةٌ
Messengers before me have come to you. 3: 183	12 قَدْ جَاءَكُمْ رُسُلٌ مِّن قَبْلِى
And indeed Our messengers came (to) Ibrahim with the good news. 11: 69	13 ■ وَلَقَدْ جَاءَتْ رُسُلُنَا إِبْرَاهِيمَ بِالْبُشْرَى
O Prophet! When the believing women come (to) you... 60: 12	14 يَـٰٓأَيُّهَا النَّبِىُّ إِذَا جَاءَكَ الْمُؤْمِنَاتُ
And the brothers of Yusuf came and entered unto him and he recognized them. 12: 58	15 ■ وَجَاءَ إِخْوَةُ يُوسُفَ فَدَخَلُوا عَلَيْهِ فَعَرَفَهُمْ

Notes for text above

■ *Lines 3, 4, 5, 7 and 8*: The words 'We' and 'Our' refer to Allah. In the Qur'an, Allah frequently refers to Himself as 'We' but this does not in any way affect the fact that Allah is One.

■ *Lines 7, 8 and 13*: لَقَدْ is a combination of the لـ of emphasis and قَدْ . To emphasize that an action is complete, the particle قَدْ or لَقَدْ is placed before the past tense verb. قَدْ with the past tense of the verb sometimes conveys the sense of the Past Perfect in English - as in قَدْ كَتَبَ - he **had** written.

قَدْ is one of the many particles which control verbs in Arabic and help to convey precise tenses. The actual tense of a verb, however, has to be determined by the context in which it is used.

■ *Lines 15:* The word يُوسُفَ is genitive. See Note for line 2, Unit 16.

Unit 16

The verb past tense: person

Person

As with pronouns, we also use the expressions 1st person, 2nd person or 3rd person when we describe any form of the verb in Arabic.

3rd person

The 3rd person is the person **spoken about**: *he, she, it,* or *they* in English.

In Arabic, the 3rd person may be: *he, she, they two* (m), *they two* (f), *they* (m. pl.) or *they* (f.pl.).

Notice in Arabic that there are four forms of the verb meaning 'they + verb':

كَتَبُوا They (m. p.) wrote.   كَتَبَا They (m.d.) wrote.

كَتَبْنَ They (m. f.) wrote.   كَتَبَتَا They (f. d.) wrote.

The masculine plural form is used for males and also for mixed groups of males and females.

2nd person

The 2nd person is the person being **spoken to**: *you.* In English, the word 'you' may refer to a male or female, to one person or a group of people. In Arabic, we have already learnt that there are five pronouns meaning 'you' and there are also five forms of the verb which refer to 'you', depending on whether you are masculine or feminine, singular, dual or plural:

كَتَبْتُم You (m. p.) wrote.   كَتَبْتَ You (m. s.) wrote

كَتَبْتُنَّ You (f. p.) wrote.   كَتَبْتِ You (f. s.) wrote

The masculine and feminine dual is كَتَبْتُمَا , You (m. & f. d.) wrote.

Hint: The verbs in the second person past tense all have the same endings as their respective separate pronouns. Repeating each verb with its pronoun may help in memorizing:

أَنْتُم كَتَبْتُم   أَنْتَ كَتَبْتَ

أَنْتُنَّ كَتَبْتُنَّ   أَنْتِ كَتَبْتِ

For the m.& f. dual, the pronoun with the verb is أَنْتُمَا :

1st person

The first person is the person **speaking**: *I, We.*

Here, as in English, there is no distinguishing between masculine and feminine. There is also no distinction between the dual and the plural.

كَتَبْتُ – I (m. & f.) wrote;   كَتَبْنَا - We (m. & f. dual and plural) wrote.

Reflecting on water

In the words of lines 4 and 5 opposite , Allah asks us to reflect on or think about the water we drink. Several verses of the Qur'an deal with the water cycle and the uses of water. Water is a crucial part of Allah's sustenance (rizq) to His creation. When we think of and use water, we are thankful to God and acknowledge His creative power and grace.

As if you see Him

The word إِحْسَان is often translated simply as 'good' or 'goodness'. It also means excellence and implies the doing of something to the best of one's ability. According to a hadith (saying of the Prophet Muhammad, peace be on him), ihsan is 'that you should worship God as if you see Him, for while you do not see Him, He surely sees you'.

He said: Did you know what you did...	1 ■	قَالَ هَلْ عَلِمْتُمْ مَا فَعَلْتُمْ
...with Yusuf and his brother? 12: 89	2 ■	بِيُوسُفَ وَأَخِيهِ
You have disbelieved after your (attaining) faith. 9: 66	3 ■	قَدْ كَفَرْتُمْ بَعْدَ إِيمَانِكُمْ
So have you seen the water...	4 ■	أَفَرَأَيْتُمُ الْمَاءَ
which you drink? 56: 67	5 ■	الَّذِى تَشْرَبُونَ
So have you seen the one who has disbelieved in Our signs? 19: 77	6 ■	أَرَأَيْتَ الَّذِى كَفَرَ بِآيَاتِنَا
Is the recompense of good (anything) but good? 55: 60	7	هَلْ جَزَاءُ الْإِحْسَانِ إِلَّا الْإِحْسَانُ
So have you found what ...	8	فَهَلْ وَجَدتُّمْ مَا
your Lord promised (to be) true? 7: 44	9	وَعَدَ رَبُّكُمْ حَقًّا
And she said (to Yusuf): 'Come out before them.'	10 ■	وَقَالَتِ اخْرُجْ عَلَيْهِنَّ
And when they saw him, they marvelled greatly at him...	11 ■	فَلَمَّا رَأَيْنَهُ أَكْبَرْنَهُ
and cut their hands...	12	وَقَطَّعْنَ أَيْدِيَهُنَّ
and said, 'May God save us!'	13	وَقُلْنَ حَاشَ لِلَّهِ
This is not a human being...	14	مَا هَٰذَا بَشَرٌ
This is nothing but a noble angel. 12: 31	15	إِنْ هَٰذَا إِلَّا مَلَكٌ كَرِيمٌ

to drink	شَرَبَ / يَشْرَبُ
to cut	قَطَعَ / يَقْطَعُ
God save us!	حَاشَ لِلَّه
a human being, human beings	بَشَرٌ
an angel	مَلَكٌ

Notes for text above

■ **Lines 1, 4 & 6:** To introduce a question, أَ or هَلْ is used. They are referred to as interrogative particles. In the Qur'an أَ is used more frequently than هَلْ .

■ **Line 2:** The word يُوسُفَ is genitive because it is controlled by the preposition بِ . Some words, including many proper names, have only one form for the accusative and genitive.

Examples: إِبْرَاهِيمَ ، إِسْرَائِيلَ ، مَرْيَمَ .

■ **Line 5:** تَشْرَبُونَ - you (2.m.p.) drink - is present tense. See Unit 21. **Line 8:** In وَجَدتُّمْ , the sukun which should be on the dal is omitted and a shaddah is placed on the ta' for ease in pronunciation.

■ **Line 10:** اخْرُجْ is imperative, (m.s.). See Unit 25.

■ **Line 11:** The word أَكْبَرْنَهُ is translated 'they marvelled greatly at him' - lit. they (f.p.) considered him great. **Line 15:** إِنْ - a negative particle followed by إِلَّا = 'nothing ...but'.

Unit 17

The verb past tense: active & passive

A verb is **active** when its subject is the doer of the action.

A verb is **passive** when its subject is acted upon.

Verbs are either active or passive.

So far we have been dealing with Arabic verbs in the past tense which are active. A verb is active when its subject is the doer of the action.

A verb is passive when its subject is acted upon.

In the following sentence,

خَلَقَ اللَّهُ الْأَرْضَ - God created the earth

the verb خَلَقَ is active. The subject, اللَّهُ , is the doer of the action.

In the following sentence,

خُلِقَ الْإِنْسَانُ - The human being was created.

the verb خُلِقَ meaning 'was created' is passive. The subject, الْإِنْسَانُ , is acted upon.

The verb in English is easily recognized as passive because it is a combination of 'was' + 'created'. The verbs in sentences like 'I am created', 'We are created', 'They were created' are all passive.

The passive of the past tense simple verb in Arabic is on the pattern of خُلِقَ . The first root letter takes a dammah and the second takes a kasrah.

| **Active** | قَتَلَتْ she killed | ذَكَرَ he mentioned |
| **Passive** | قُتِلَتْ she was killed | ذُكِرَ he was mentioned |

The suffixes or endings of passive verbs are the same as those of past tense active verbs given in the previous units.

Note: The word إِبِل in line 10 opposite is normally taken to mean 'she-camels'. Muhammad Asad (*The Meaning of the Qur'an*, p. 949) has pointed out that the word has a rarer meaning of 'clouds bearing rain-water'. This better fits the context which refers to the skies, mountains and the earth.

weak	ضَعِيفٌ
female child	الْمَوْءُودَةُ
to ask	سَأَلَ
to tremble	وَجِلَ
fasting	صِيَامٌ
Stand firm!	اِسْتَقِمْ

Unwanted

الْمَوْءُودَةُ refers, In line 7 opposite, to the 'unwanted' girl child who is murdered by parents or others and who in the hereafter will point its accusing finger at its murderer. The Qur'an condemns this practice of infanticide. Those who are responsible for this heinous crime will be brought to account on the day of judgment. The appalling practice is not just of the past. In fact as a result of genetic screening and social engineering, and the rampant spread of abortions worldwide through the 'pro-choice' lobby, this practice is now on a far vaster scale than it has even been in the past.

He created the human being. 55: 3	١ خَلَقَ الإِنْسَانَ
The human being was created weak. 4: 28	٢ خُلِقَ الإِنْسَانُ ضَعِيفًا
He gathered wealth. 104: 2	٣ جَمَعَ مَالًا
So the sorcerers were gathered. 26: 38	٤ ■ فَجُمِعَ السَّحَرَةُ
And Dawud killed Jalut. 2: 251	٥ وَقَتَلَ دَاوُودُ جَالُوتَ
And whoever has been killed unjustly... 17: 33	٦ وَمَنْ قُتِلَ مَظْلُومًا
And when the female babe is asked: for what sin was she killed? 81: 9	٧ وَإِذَا الْمَوْءُودَةُ سُئِلَتْ بِأَىّ ذَنْبٍ قُتِلَتْ
Perish the human being! How ungrateful is he! 80: 17	٨ ■ قُتِلَ الإِنْسَانُ مَا أَكْفَرَهُ
Permission (to fight) has been given to those who are being fought because they were wronged. 22: 39	٩ أُذِنَ لِلَّذِينَ يُقَاتَلُونَ بِأَنَّهُمْ ظُلِمُوا
Do they not look at the clouds - how they were created? 88: 13	١٠ أَفَلَا يَنْظُرُونَ إِلَى الإِبِلِ كَيْفَ خُلِقَتْ
When Allah is mentioned, their hearts tremble. 22: 35	١١ ■ إِذَا ذُكِرَ اللَّهُ وَجِلَتْ قُلُوبُهُمْ
Fasting has been prescribed for you (lit. on you). 2: 183	١٢ كُتِبَ عَلَيْكُمُ الصِّيَامُ
And if you were killed in the path of God or were to die...	١٣ ■ وَلَئِنْ قُتِلْتُمْ فِى سَبِيلِ اللَّهِ أَوْ مُتُّمْ
...then forgiveness from God and His grace is better than whatever (wealth) they amass. 3: 157	١٤ لَمَغْفِرَةٌ مِنَ اللَّهِ وَرَحْمَةٌ خَيْرٌ مِمَّا يَجْمَعُونَ
And stand firm as you were commanded. 32: 15	١٥ وَاسْتَقِمْ كَمَا أُمِرْتَ

Notes for text above

■ *Line 4:* The verb, whether active or passive, is singular when it is the first word in a sentence. This is so whether the subject of the sentence is singular, dual or plural. For example, the subject السَّحَرَةُ the sorcerers, is plural but the verb جُمِعَ is singular.

■ *Line 8:* The verb قُتِلَ is used to express a wish. The past tense of the verb in Arabic, whether active or passive, is sometimes used to express a wish. An

example of this - not from the Qur'an - is رَحِمَهُ اللَّهُ - *may God have mercy on him.*

The construction مَا أَكْفَرَهُ is used to express the exclamation: *How ungrateful is he!* It is made up of مَا + comparative adjective + the pronoun ـهُ (For comparative adjectives, see Unit 18.)

■ *Line 11.* This is a conditional sentence (see Unit 40) introduced by the particle إِذَا , meaning '*if*' or '*when*'.

■ *Line 13.* لَئِنْ = إِنْ + لَ

In English, adjectives like big, bigger and biggest are called positive, comparative and superlative respectively.

In Arabic, there is only one form for the comparative and the superlative.

Two verbs which occur very frequently in the Qur'an are قَالَ and كَانَ in their various forms.

They are called hollow verbs. The alif in قال and كان stands for the letter و . So: the root letters of قال are ق و ل ; the root letters of كان are ك و ن .

This means that if you are looking up قال in a dictionary, you will need to look under ق و ل and not (ق ا ل). The second root letter 'waw' is also important when we come to deal with the present tense of قَالَ .

Below is given the full conjugation of قَالَ in the past tense. You will see that the alif is dropped in all the 1st and 2nd person forms, and in the feminine plural 3rd person. Whenever the alif is dropped, the ق takes a dammah.

Plural	Dual	Singular	
قَالُوا	قَالَا	قَالَ	3.m.
قُلْنَ	قَالَتَا	قَالَتْ	3.f.
قُلْتُمْ	قُلْتُمَا	قُلْتَ	2.m.
قُلْتُنَّ	قُلْتُمَا	قُلْتِ	2.f.
قُلْنَا	قُلْنَا	قُلْتُ	1. m & f.

The passive of قَالَ is قِيلَ , *it has been said, it is said.*

Adjectives: comparative & superlative

In line 1 opposite, the word أَكْبَرُ meaning 'bigger' or 'greater', is the comparative form of the adjective كَبِيرٌ meaning 'big' or 'great'. Many adjectives follow the same pattern. In English, we use the terms <u>positive</u>, <u>comparative</u> and <u>superlative</u> for adjectives used for comparing. For example, <u>big</u>, <u>bigger</u> and <u>biggest</u> are positive, comparative and superlative respectively.

In Arabic, to form the comparative of a masculine adjective, an alif is added before the first root letter. A sukun is then placed on the first root letter. The second root letter takes a fat-hah. **Read from right to left.**

	Comparative		Positive
bigger	أَكْبَرُ	big	كَبِيرٌ
smaller	أَصْغَرُ	small	صَغِيرٌ
nearer	أَقْرَبُ	near	قَرِيبٌ
more	أَكْثَرُ	many	كَثِيرٌ
greater	أَعْظَمُ	great	عَظِيمٌ

We hear and we obey
The response of a believer to Divine guidance contained in the Qur'an is to accept and follow it. But this is not robotic behaviour. It is based on the clear consciousness of the absolute knowledge, wisdom and justice of God Who knows what is best for His creatures. Each person has a duty to use his or her God-given reason to ponder and reflect.

Arabic uses the comparative form for the superlative as well. So the word أَكْبَرُ can mean both '<u>bigger</u>' and '<u>biggest</u>'. You can tell from the context whether an adjective is comparative or superlative.

The feminine of كَبِيرٌ is كَبِيرَةٌ , the comparative form of which is كُبْرَى which means '<u>greater</u>' or '<u>greatest</u>' as in الآيَةُ الْكُبْرَى - the greatest sign.

English	#	Arabic
He said: This (is) my Lord. This (is) greater. 6: 78	1	قَالَ هَذَا رَبِّي هَذَا أَكْبَرُ
He said: I am better than he. 7: 12	2	قَالَ أَنَا خَيْرٌ مِنْهُ
She said: It is from God. 3: 37	3	قَالَتْ هُوَ مِنْ عِنْدِ اللَّهِ
She said: My Sustainer! Indeed I have wronged myself. 27: 44	4	قَالَتْ رَبِّ إِنِّي ظَلَمْتُ نَفْسِي
They both said: Our Sustainer! We have wronged ourselves. 7: 23	5	قَالَا رَبَّنَا ظَلَمْنَا أَنْفُسَنَا
They (f.) both said: Our father (is) an old man. 28: 23	6	قَالَتَا أَبُونَا شَيْخٌ كَبِيرٌ
They said: We heard and disobeyed. 2: 93	7	قَالُوا سَمِعْنَا وَعَصَيْنَا
They said: We heard and obeyed. 2: 285	8	وَقَالُوا سَمِعْنَا وَأَطَعْنَا
Did you say to people...? 5: 116	9	أَأَنْتَ قُلْتَ لِلنَّاسِ ...
I did not say to them...	10	مَا قُلْتُ لَهُمْ ...
except what You commanded me. 5:117	11	إِلَّا مَا أَمَرْتَنِي بِهِ
And behold! We said to the angels... 2: 34	12	وَإِذْ قُلْنَا لِلْمَلَائِكَةِ
And behold, you said: O Musa,	13	وَإِذْ قُلْتُمْ يَا مُوسَى
we shall not bear one (type of) food. 2: 61	14	لَنْ نَصْبِرَ عَلَى طَعَامٍ وَاحِدٍ
And when it is said to them: Believe, as people have believed... 2: 13	15	وَإِذَا قِيلَ لَهُمْ آمِنُوا كَمَا آمَنَ النَّاسُ

Vocabulary: شَيْخٌ an old man — عَصَى to disobey — أَطَاعَ to obey — طَعَامٌ food

Notes for text above

Line 10: The first مَا negates the verb: قُلْتُ - I said; مَا قُلْتُ - I did not say.

Line 11: The مَا means 'what'. بِهِ, meaning 'with it' must be included in the Arabic but is not translated in the English.

Line 14: The word لَنْ means 'shall not'. It is followed by a verb in the subjunctive. See Unit 23.

Line 15: The word آمِنُوا is imperative plural. Notice the kasrah with the mim. See Unit 33.

Finding out: Use a translation of the Qur'an to find out the following: Who is the speaker in line 1, line 2, line 3, line 4 and line 10? Who are the speakers in line 5, line 6 and lines 13-14? Describe the context of each of these lines.

Unit 19

The past tense of كَانَ

The **noun** of كَانَ is in the nominative.

The **predicate** of كَانَ is in the accusative.

Below is a chart with the full conjugation of the verb كَانَ in the past tense. It follows the same pattern as that of قَالَ .

Plural	Dual	Singular	
كَانُوا	كَانَا	كَانَ	3.m.
كُنَّ	كَانَتَا	كَانَتْ	3.f.
كُنْتُمْ	كُنْتُمَا	كُنْتَ	2.m.
كُنْتُنَّ	كُنْتُمَا	كُنْتِ	2.f.
كُنَّا	كُنَّا	كُنْتُ	1.m.f.

The 3rd person feminine plural كُنَّ is a contraction of كُنَّ

The 1st person plural كُنَّا is a contraction of كُنَّا .

The 'noun' of ka̲na and the 'predicate' of ka̲na

Study the following sentence:

كَانَ النَّاسُ أُمَّةً وَاحِدَةً - Mankind was one nation.

In this sentence, the word النَّاسُ is called in Arabic 'the noun of كَانَ '. The word النَّاسُ is nominative, ending with a dammah. The noun of كَانَ is in the nominative case .

The word أُمَّةً is the predicate or خَبَر of كَانَ . It is accusative, ending with fat-hah. The predicate of كَانَ is in the accusative case.

(The word وَاحِدَةً is an adjective of أُمَّةً and agrees with it in gender and case.)

Below are more examples with ka̲na. Notice that all the nouns of ka̲na are nominative and all the predicates are accusative. **Read from right to left.**

Predicate of kana	Noun of kana	kana	
أُمَّةً	النَّاسُ	كَانَ	Mankind was one nation.
غَفُورًا	اللَّهُ	كَانَ	God has been Forgiving.
مُؤْمِنِينَ		كَانُوا	They were believers.
يَهُودِيًّا	إِبْرَاهِيمُ	مَا كَانَ	Ibrahim was not a Jew.
صَادِقِينَ		إِنْ كُنْتُمْ	If you were truthful.

Notes for text on opposite page:

Line 7: The word مُسْلِمِينَ is accusative because it is the predicate of كَانُوا .

Line 9: The word خَيْرَ is accusative because it is the predicate of كُنْتُمْ .

Line 10: The word ظَالِمِينَ is accusative because it is the predicate of كُنَّا .

Line 14: The word تُرَابًا is accusative because it is the predicate of كُنْتُ .

Line 15: The word اللَّهُ is nominative because it is the noun of كَانَ .

The one who conceals
The word 'kafir' is the active participle of the verb kafara which has the basic meaning of 'to conceal' or 'to cover up'. A kafir may be described as one who 'covers up' his natural state of goodness and virtue and denies or rejects the natural belief in one God. A kafir is also one who is ungrateful for all the favours which God has bestowed on the human being.
The word kafir has two plurals: kafirun and kuffar. In one instance in the Qur'an (surah al-Hadid, 57: 20), the word kuffar is used to mean 'tillers' of the soil, people who 'cover up' seed with soil.

Mankind was one nation. 2: 213	1 ■ كَانَ النَّاسُ أُمَّةً وَاحِدَةً
And he was from among the disbelievers. 2: 34	2 وَكَانَ مِنَ الْكَافِرِينَ
And indeed she was from a disbelieving folk. 28: 47	3 إِنَّهَا كَانَت مِن قَوْمٍ كَافِرِينَ
And she was one of the devout. 66: 12	4 وَكَانَت مِنَ الْقَانِتِينَ
(There is) no god but You. Glory be to You. 21: 87	5 لَا إِلٰهَ إِلَّا أَنْتَ سُبْحَانَكَ
Indeed, I have been one of the wrongdoers. 21: 87	6 إِنِّى كُنْتُ مِنَ الظَّالِمِينَ
They were Muslims (submitting to God). 43: 69	7 كَانُوا مُسْلِمِينَ
They were before that doers of good. 51: 16	8 كَانُوا قَبْلَ ذٰلِكَ مُحْسِنِينَ
You are the best community produced for mankind... 3: 110	9 كُنْتُمْ خَيْرَ أُمَّةٍ أُخْرِجَت لِلنَّاسِ
They said: Glory be to our Sustainer! Indeed we, we were wrong-doers. 68: 29	10 قَالُوا سُبْحَانَ رَبِّنَا إِنَّا كُنَّا ظَالِمِينَ
So He expelled them both from where they were. 2: 36	11 فَأَخْرَجَهُمَا مِمَّا كَانَا فِيهِ
And if (it were) not for God's favour on you and His mercy,	12 ■ وَلَوْ لَا فَضْلُ اللَّهِ عَلَيْكُمْ وَرَحْمَتُهُ
you would certainly have been among the losers. 2: 64	13 لَكُنْتُمْ مِنَ الْخَاسِرِينَ
And the unbeliever would say, 'O! Would that I were dust.' 78: 40	14 ■ وَقَالَ الْكَافِرُ يٰلَيْتَنِى كُنْتُ تُرَابًا
And God has been Forgiving, Merciful. 4: 96	15 ■ وَكَانَ اللَّهُ غَفُورًا رَحِيمًا

Notes for text above

■ *Line 1:* The word 'ummah' (plural: umam) means community or nation. It is used in the Qur'an to refer to the community of believers or the universal Muslim community which is described as a middle community. Other species in creation (such as birds) are also referred to in the Qur'an as 'umam' or 'communities'.

■ *Line 12:* لَوْ meaning 'if' introduces a conditional setence. This is why the following لَكُنْتُمْ is translated as 'you would certainly have been' . The

initial لَ is the lam of emphasis.

■ *Line 14:* يٰلَيْتَنِى is a combination of لَيْتَ + نِى + يـ meaning ' O!, would that I ...'.

■ *Line 15:* Note that the verb كَانَ refers not only to the past but to the present as well. It has the sense of 'was' and 'continues to be'. The past form of the verb in Arabic is often used in a past and present continuous sense. It is important to look at the context in which a verb is used to determine its tense.

Unit 20

The verb - the present tense

The Arabic word for the past tense is الـْمَاضِى

The Arabic word for the present tense is الـْمُضَارِع

So far, we have been dealing with the Past Tense of the simple verb in Arabic. In this Unit, we will introduce the Present Tense which in fact is used to represent all present tenses and the future.

The Present Tense is formed by adding prefixes and suffixes to the root word. The **prefix** in this case is a letter with its vowel which is **added before** the first root letter.
The **suffix** may be **(i)** a vowel or **(ii)** letters and vowels **added after** the root letters.

In the following example, see how the Present Tense (3.m.) is formed from the root word. **Read from right to left.**

Present Tense 3.m.p.	Present Tense 3.m.s.	Root Word 3.m.s.
يَكْتُبُونَ	يَكْتُبُ	كَتَبَ
they write, they are writing	he writes, he is writing	he wrote

You will notice that for the above example in the present tense:

(i) the prefix يَ is added to both the singular and plural masculine 3rd person.
(ii) the first root letter كـ has a sukun.
(iii) the second root letter ـتـ has a dammah. In some verbs, the second root letter may have a fat-hah or a kasrah, for example:

جَعَلَ / يَجْعَلُ he made/he makes . يَجْعَلُ has a fat-hah on the second root letter.
رَجَعَ / يَرْجِعُ he returned/he returns . يَرْجِعُ has a kasrah.

For each verb, you need to learn the present form with the root word to ensure that you use the correct vowel on the second root letter.
(iv) the singular form ends with a dammah.
(v) the plural form ends with ـُونَ .

Study some of the singular and plural parts of the present tense conjugation of the verb سَجَدَ below. Read from right to left.

	Plural		Singular		
they prostrate they are prostrating	يَسْجُدُونَ		يَسْجُدُ	he prostrates he is prostrating	3.m.
you prostrate you are prostrating	تَسْجُدُونَ		تَسْجُدُ	you prostrate you are prostrating	2.m.
we prostrate we are prostrating	نَسْجُدُ		أَسْجُدُ	I prostrate I am prostrating	1.m.&f.

You will notice that:

• The prefix تَ refers here to the second person - **you.**
• The prefix أ refers to I; the prefix نَ refers to **we.**
• The first root letter س has a sukun throughout.
• The 3.m.p. and 2.m.p. forms both end with ـُونَ .

Note that the present tense conjugation of the verbs above is in the **indicative mood.** This will be explained in the next Unit.

Appropriate use
An'am (line 12 opposite) refers to all livestock - cattle, goats, sheep, camels. In them are many benefits (manafi') for people, providing food, drink, clothing, transport. They are to be cared for as creatures of God for they are communities ('umam') like you. They are not to be ill-treated and abused. At the same time, animals should not be accorded any supernatural status or qualities.
Surah 6 of the Qur'an is called Al-An'am. In verses 136ff, the practice of regarding cattle as sacred is condemned as are all tendencies to attribute Divine qualities to created beings or imaginary powers.

He creates what you do not know. 16: 18	1	يَخْلُقُ مَا لَا تَعْلَمُونَ
He knows whatever enters in the earth and whatever comes out of it,	2 ■	يَعْلَمُ مَا يَلِجُ فِى الْأَرْضِ وَ مَا يَخْرُجُ مِنْهَا
and what descends from the sky and what ascends to it,	3 ■	وَمَا يَنْزِلُ مِنَ السَّمَاءِ وَمَا يَعْرُجُ فِيهَا
and He is with you wherever you may be (lit. you have been) 57: 4	4	وَهُوَ مَعَكُمْ أَيْنَ مَا كُنْتُمْ
And God is All-Seeing of whatever you do. 57: 4	5	وَاللَّهُ بِمَا تَعْمَلُونَ بَصِيرٌ
Indeed God does not wrong (even) the weight of an atom. 4: 40	6	إِنَّ اللَّهَ لَا يَظْلِمُ مِثْقَالَ ذَرَّةٍ
They do not know the Truth. 21: 24	7	لَا يَعْلَمُونَ الْحَقَّ
They shall have their reward with their Sustainer ...	8 ■	لَهُمْ أَجْرُهُمْ عِنْدَ رَبِّهِمْ
and no fear shall be on them and they shall not grieve. 2: 262	9 ■	وَلَا خَوْفٌ عَلَيْهِمْ وَلَا هُمْ يَحْزَنُونَ
He said: Indeed, I know what you do not know. 2: 30	10	قَالَ إِنِّى أَعْلَمُ مَا لَا تَعْلَمُونَ
Have you seen the water that you drink? 56: 68	11	أَرَأَيْتُمُ الْمَاءَ الَّذِى تَشْرَبُونَ
And the cattle - He created them. For you, in them, is warmth...	12 ■	وَالْأَنْعَامَ خَلَقَهَا لَكُمْ فِيهَا دِفْءٌ
and (other) uses, and of them you eat. 16: 5	13	وَمَنَافِعُ وَمِنْهَا تَأْكُلُونَ
I do not worship what you worship. 109: 2	14	لَا أَعْبُدُ مَا تَعْبُدُونَ
You alone we worship. 1: 5	15 ■	إِيَّاكَ نَعْبُدُ

Notes for text above

■ *Line 2:* The verb يَلِجُ is the present tense of وَلَجَ *to enter, penetrate* and is known as a 'weak verb'.

■ *Line 3:* يَعْرُجُ is present tense of عَرَجَ *to ascend*. From this comes the word مِعْرَاجٌ *a ladder*.

■ *Line 8 & 9:* لَهُمْ *for them*, also means 'they have'. Here it refers to the future and so is translated as 'they shall have'. يَحْزَنُونَ 'they shall not grieve' is

an example of the Arabic present form which refers to the future.

■ *Line 12:* أَنْعَام is grammatically feminine singular and so the pronoun هَا is used for it.

■ *Line 15:* For إِيَّاكَ see note on line 5, Unit 7 . Pronouns attached to إِيَّا are normally placed before the verb.

In the last Unit, we mentioned that the middle root letter in the Present Tense verb may take a dammah, fat-hah or a kasrah. Below we give an example of each with the full conjugation of the verb in the present tense.

You will notice throughout that:

i. the prefix يَـ represents the 3rd person.

ii. the prefix تَـ represents the 2nd person (with the exception of the 3rd person fem. singular and dual).

iii. the prefix أَ represents **I**.

iv. the prefix نَـ represents **We**.

v. the first root letter in a regular verb takes a sukun throughout.

The past form of the verb is sometimes referred in English to as the **Perfect**.

The present form of the verb is sometimes referred to as the **Imperfect**.

The **indicative** is used to make a statement about an action in the present or the future, e.g. he writes, he is writing, he shall write.

Plural	Dual	Singular	
يَكْتُبُونَ	يَكْتُبَانِ	يَكْتُبُ	3.m.
يَكْتُبْنَ	تَكْتُبَانِ	تَكْتُبُ	3.f.
تَكْتُبُونَ	تَكْتُبَانِ	تَكْتُبُ	2.m.
تَكْتُبْنَ	تَكْتُبَانِ	تَكْتُبِينَ	2.f.
نَكْتُبُ	نَكْتُبُ	أَكْتُبُ	1.m. & f.

The verb يَعْلَمُ in the present takes a fat-hah on the middle root letter.

Plural	Dual	Singular	
يَعْلَمُونَ	يَعْلَمَانِ	يَعْلَمُ	3.m.
يَعْلَمْنَ	تَعْلَمَانِ	تَعْلَمُ	3.f.
تَعْلَمُونَ	تَعْلَمَانِ	تَعْلَمُ	2.m.
تَعْلَمْنَ	تَعْلَمَانِ	تَعْلَمِينَ	2.f.
نَعْلَمُ	نَعْلَمُ	أَعْلَمُ	1.m. & f.

The verb يَرْجِعُ in the present takes a kasrah with the middle root letter.

Plural	Dual	Singular	
يَرْجِعُونَ	يَرْجِعَانِ	يَرْجِعُ	3.m.
يَرْجِعْنَ	تَرْجِعَانِ	تَرْجِعُ	3.f.
تَرْجِعُونَ	تَرْجِعَانِ	تَرْجِعُ	2.m.
تَرْجِعْنَ	تَرْجِعَانِ	تَرْجِعِينَ	2.f.
نَرْجِعُ	نَرْجِعُ	أَرْجِعُ	1.m. & f.

Let us give thanks
God has divided people into two streams, the people of gratitude (*shukr*) and the people of ingratitude (*kufr*). *'Indeed, We have shown him (the human being) the way - whether he is grateful or ungrateful (is up to him).' 76: 3* Ingratitude, conceit, arrogance, rejection of the truth and ultimate humiliation are all part of the same stream. God has explained in the Qur'an that the only people who truly worship Him are those who give thanks. Those who are not among the people of gratitude therefore are not among the people of 'ibadah or worship. *'And be grateful to God, if indeed it is Him you worship (2: 172).'*

Indicative Mood

The present tense conjugation of the verb above is in the **indicative mood** (مَرْفُوع). You will notice that in this mood: (i) the last letter of all the singular forms (except 2nd person feminine) and the 1st person plural has a dammah.

(ii) the dual forms end with انِ .

(iii) the masculine plural forms (2nd and 3rd persons) end with ـُونَ .

(iv) the feminine plural forms end with نَ preceded by a letter with a sukun:

It is important to remember points (i) , (ii) and (iii) above, especially when we come to deal with the verb in its other moods - the subjunctive (مَنْصُوب), the jussive (مَجْزُوم) and the imperative (أَمْر) .

Do you command people with righteousness and you forget yourselves...	1	أَتَأْمُرُونَ النَّاسَ بِالْبِرِّ وَتَنْسَوْنَ أَنْفُسَكُمْ
while you read the Book (of God)? Would you not use your reason? 2: 44	2 ■	وَأَنْتُمْ تَتْلُونَ الْكِتَابَ أَفَلَا تَعْقِلُونَ
You are the best community produced for (the benefit of) mankind - you command ...	3	كُنْتُمْ خَيْرَ أُمَّةٍ أُخْرِجَتْ لِلنَّاسِ تَأْمُرُونَ
the good and forbid the evil and you believe in God. 3: 110	4	بِالْمَعْرُوفِ وَتَنْهَوْنَ عَنِ الْمُنْكَرِ وَتُؤْمِنُونَ بِاللَّهِ
Indeed God is the Possessor of bounty for all people ...	5	إِنَّ اللَّهَ لَذُو فَضْلٍ عَلَى النَّاسِ
but most people do not give thanks. 2: 243	6	وَلَـٰكِنَّ أَكْثَرَ النَّاسِ لَا يَشْكُرُونَ
God has promised the believing men and the believing women gardens...	7	وَعَدَ اللَّهُ الْمُؤْمِنِينَ وَالْمُؤْمِنَاتِ جَنَّاتٍ
through which rivers flow. 9: 72	8 ■	تَجْرِي مِنْ تَحْتِهَا الْأَنْهَارُ
In these two (gardens), two springs will flow. 55: 50	9 ■	فِيهِمَا عَيْنَانِ تَجْرِيَانِ
The shoots and the trees both prostrate. 55: 6	10 ■	وَالنَّجْمُ وَالشَّجَرُ يَسْجُدَانِ
And the cattle - He created them. For you in them is warmth...	11	وَالْأَنْعَامَ خَلَقَهَا لَكُمْ فِيهَا دِفْءٌ
and (other) uses and of them you eat. 16: 5	12	وَمَنَافِعُ وَمِنْهَا تَأْكُلُونَ
and they carry your loads to (many) a land. 16: 7	13	وَتَحْمِلُ أَثْقَالَكُمْ إِلَى بَلَدٍ
So she (Maryam) came with him (to) her people carrying him...	14 ■	فَأَتَتْ بِهِ قَوْمَهَا تَحْمِلُهُ
They said: O Maryam, you have come (with) a strange thing. 19: 27	15	قَالُوا يَا مَرْيَمُ لَقَدْ جِئْتِ شَيْئًا فَرِيًّا

Notes for text above

■ *Line 2:* The letter و is translated here as 'while'. This waw is known as the *waw al-hal* and points to an action taking place at the same time as another.

■ *Line 8:* The verb تَجْرِي is feminine singular of جرى *to run*. Its subject is أَنْهَار which is the broken plural of نَهَر; it is thus considered feminine singular. تَحْتَهَا literally means 'underneath them' (i.e. gardens)

but is translated above as 'through them'.

■ *Line 9:* The word تَجْرِيَانِ has a future sense.

■ *Line 10:* نَجْم is normally translated as 'stars'. It may also mean 'shoots' from the ground.

■ *Line 14:* أَتَتْ, *she came* - is the feminine of أَتَى which takes a direct object. *She* refers to Maryam, may God be pleased with her. The ـهِ in بِهِ refers to the baby 'Isa (Jesus).

The conjugation of irregular verbs needs to be learnt separately.

At this stage, **irregular verbs** are best studied in the context in which they are used.

The verb كَتَبَ is described as a regular Form I verb.

In sentence 1 opposite, the verb يَشَاءُ *he wishes*, is the present tense of شَاءَ which is an irregular Form I verb.

A verb is irregular

i.   if one of its root letters is a weak letter, i.e. ا , و , or ي .

ii. If the second and third root letters are the same, e.g. ضَلَّ *he went astray*.

شَاءَ is an irregular verb because it has an alif as its middle root letter.

The irregular verb رَأَى / يَرَى , *he saw /he sees* is used often in the Qur'an in its various forms. In the past tense, it is on the whole conjugated regularly.

However, in the present, the middle root letter - the alif with the hamza - is dropped. The first root letter - the ر then takes a fat-hah.

	Present		Past	
he sees	يَرَى		رَأَى	he saw
she sees	تَرَى		رَأَتْ	she saw
you (m.s.) see	تَرَى		رَأَيْتَ	you (m.s.) saw
you (f.s.) see	تَرِينَ		رَأَيْتِ	you (f.s.) saw
I see	أَرَى		رَأَيْتُ	1 (m. & f.) saw

The conjugation of irregular verbs needs to be learnt separately. At this stage, these verbs are probably best studied in the context in which they are used.

The Future

(a) The future is expressed by the present form on its own - the context will tell you if the verb refers to the future. In line 11 opposite, the verb يَجْمَعُ has the meaning '*He shall gather*'. In line 14, the word تَكْسِبُ means '*it shall earn*' .

(b) The future is also expressed by سَوْفَ which is placed before the present form of the verb: سَوْفَ تَعْلَمُونَ , *you shall know*.

The particle سَوْفَ is also used in its shortened form سَـ as an attached prefix: e.g. in line 12 opposite, سَيَجْعَلُ اللَّهُ , *God shall make.*

He eats and walks in the market-places!

The Makkans who refused to believe that Muhammad, peace be on him, was a messenger of God, tried to mock and ridicule him by saying, 'What is wrong with this messenger! He eats and walks in the market-places!' (lines 4 & 5 opposite). But the Qur'an says that even if God were to have sent down an angel as a messenger, they would still be mocking and incredulous.
The Qur'an emphasises that the Prophet Muhammad was only a human being with human needs and desires but, inspired by God, he was and remains a shining good example for human conduct and all who set their hopes in God and the Hereafter.

سُوق / أَسْوَاق	market/markets	عُسْر	difficulty
غَدًا	tomorrow	يُسْر	ease
رَأْس	head	خُبْز	bread

١	يَخْلُقُ مَا يَشَاءُ	He creates whatever He wills. 5: 17
٢	وَ تَرزُقُ مَنْ تَشَاءُ بِغَيرِ حِسَابٍ	And You provide whoever You wish without measure. 3: 27
٣	لَهُمْ مَا يَشَاءُونَ عِندَ رَبِّهِمْ	They shall have whatever they desire with their Sustainer. 39: 34
٤ ■	وَقَالُوا مَا لِهَذَا الرَّسُولِ	And they said: What is wrong with this Messenger...
٥	يَأْكُلُ الطَّعَامَ وَ يَمْشِى فِى الأَسْوَاقِ	he eats food and walks in the market-places? 25: 7
٦	إِنَّ رَبَّكَ هُوَ أَعْلَمُ مَنْ يَضِلُّ عَنْ سَبِيلِهِ	Indeed your Lord - He knows best who goes astray from His path. 6: 117
٧	إِنَّ الَّذِينَ يَضِلُّونَ عَنْ سَبِيلِ اللَّهِ لَهُمْ عَذَابٌ شَدِيدٌ	Those who go astray from God's path, they shall have a severe punishment. 38: 26
٨	إِنِّى أَرَى مَا لَا تَرَوْنَ إِنِّى أَخَافُ اللَّهَ	Indeed, I see what you do not see. Indeed, I fear God. 8: 48
٩	وَقَالَ الآخَرُ إِنِّى أَرَانِى أَحْمِلُ فَوْقَ رَأْسِى خُبْزًا	And the other said: Verily, I see myself carrying bread on my head. 12: 36
١٠ ■	وَقُلِ اعْمَلُوا فَسَيَرَى اللَّهُ عَمَلَكُمْ وَرَسُولُهُ وَالْمُؤْمِنُونَ	And say, Work! And God and His messenger and the believers will see your work. 9: 105
١١	ثُمَّ يَجْمَعُكُمْ إِلَى يومِ القِيَامَةِ	Then He shall gather you to the Day of Judgment. 45: 26
١٢	سَيَجْعَلُ اللَّهُ بَعْدَ عُسْرٍ يُسْرًا	God shall make ease after hardship. 65: 7
١٣	كَلاَّ سَوْفَ تَعْلَمُونَ ، ثُمَّ كَلاَّ سَوْفَ تَعْلَمُونَ	Nay! You shall know. Again, nay, you shall know. 102: 3-4
١٤ ■	وَمَا تَدْرِى نَفْسٌ مَاذَا تَكْسِبُ غَدًا	A person does not know what it shall earn tomorrow...
١٥ ■	وَمَا تَدْرِى نَفْسٌ بِأَىِّ أَرْضٍ تَمُوتُ	and a person does not know in which land it shall die. 31: 34

Notes for text above

■ *Line 4:* مَا followed by the preposition لَ or

لِ is an expression meaning '*What is wrong with ...?*'

or '*What is the matter with ...?*' For example

مَا لَكَ, *What's the matter with you?*

■ *Line 10:* فَ + سَـ + يَرى = فَسَيَرَى. The سَـ is

short for سَوْفَ '*will*'.

■ *Line 10:* Note that the singular verb يَرى has

multiple subjects - *Allah, His messenger, the believers.*

كَلاَّ has the sense of 'on the contrary' but is

translated by the old English word '*Nay*'.

■ *Lines 14 & 15:* The word نَفْسٌ is feminine and

therefore the verb تَدْرِى is also feminine.

Unit 23

The subjunctive

The verb in the present form has three moods: **the indicative** (مَرْفُوع), **the subjunctive** (مَنْصُوب), and **the jussive** (مَجْزُوم).

We saw in Unit 21 that present tense verbs in the indicative mood which end with a root letter has a dammah on that letter. For example, the words يَعْلَمُ and يَنْزِلُ in the sentence below are in the indicative mood. They each end with a dammah.

يَعْلَمُ مَا يَنْزِلُ مِنَ السَّمَاءِ   He knows what descends from the sky.

When the present form of the verb is controlled by certain words or particles, the endings or suffixes of the verb are affected.

In the clause below, the particle لِ *so that*, controls the verb يَعْلَمَ causing it to end in a fat-hah instead of the dammah:

لِيَعْلَمَ اللَّهُ مَن يَنصُرُه   So that Allah may know who helps Him.

The word يَعْلَمَ is said to be in the subjunctive mood (مَنْصُوب). The subjunctive is used after the following particles, which we will call 'controllers'.

أَنْ	that	أَنْ لاَ = أَلَّا	that not
لَنْ	will not, never	لِئَلَّا	so that not
لِ	in order to , so that	كَيْ	in order to , so that
حَتَّى	until, so that	كَيْلاَ	so that not

Sidebar

Slight changes are made to the indicative of the present tense Arabic verb to form **the subjunctive**.
• The subjunctive is used after the main verb in a sentence.
• One common use of the subjunctive is after verbs of commanding, wishing, fearing and the like. For example, the Arabic verb translating 'to eat' in line 1 opposite is in the subjunctive.
• Subjunctive verbs are linked to or controlled by preceding particles. We will call these particles **'controllers'**.

In English a verb in the subjunctive may sometimes be recognised by having 'should', 'would', 'may' or 'might' as part of the verb.

So that they may worship Me

The human being's reason for existence (line 7) is to 'worship' his or her Creator. This is also the purpose of other creatures. Worship ('ibādah) is Prayer and supplications. And it is much more. It is to seek useful knowledge; it is honest work; it is relaxation and lawful pleasures; it is acts of kindness and charity and resisting evil; it is concern for the earth on which we live - all done in tune with our natural disposition, in obedience to God alone, in the hope of His pleasure and in dread of His displeasure.

Conjugation table

Controllers		Singular		Dual		Plural
أَنْ	3.m.	يَكْتُبَ		يَكْتُبَا		يَكْتُبُوا
لَنْ	3.f.	تَكْتُبَ		تَكْتُبَا		يَكْتُبْنَ
إِذَنْ	2.m.	تَكْتُبَ		تَكْتُبَا		تَكْتُبُوا
حَتَّى	2.f.	تَكْتُبِي		تَكْتُبَا		تَكْتُبْنَ
كَىْ	1.m.&f.	أَكْتُبَ		نَكْتُبَ		نَكْتُبَ
لِئَلا						
أَنْ لا						
لِ						

You will notice that for the subjunctive:

(i) The forms of the verb which have no added letters after the last root letter, change the final dammah of the indicative to a fat-hah, e.g. يَكْتُبَ

(ii) The forms of the verb which end with ن preceded by a long vowel after the last root letter, lose their ن . An alif is then added after the long vowel 'u' of the 2nd and 3rd person masculine plural, e.g. يَكْتُبُوا

(iii) The second and third person plural feminine forms stay the same in the indicative, subjunctive and jussive moods.

They said: We want to eat (*lit.* that we should eat) of it. 5: 113	1 ■ قَالُوا نُرِيدُ أَنْ نَأْكُلَ مِنْهَا
Do you want to kill (*lit.* that you should kill) me as you killed someone yesterday. 28: 19	2 أَتُرِيدُ أَنْ تَقْتُلَنِي كَمَا قَتَلْتَ نَفْساً بِالْأَمْسِ
They want to get out of the fire. 5: 37	3 يُرِيدُونَ أَنْ يَخْرُجُوا مِنَ النَّارِ
So that Allah may know who helps Him and His messengers. 57: 25	4 لِيَعْلَمَ اللَّهُ مَنْ يَنْصُرُهُ وَرُسُلَهُ
That (is) so that you may know that Allah knows...	5 ذٰلِكَ لِتَعْلَمُوا أَنَّ اللَّهَ يَعْلَمُ
...whatever is in the heavens and whatever is in the earth. 5: 97	6 مَا فِي السَّمٰوٰتِ وَمَا فِي الْأَرْضِ
I have not created jinn and human beings except that they should worship Me. 51: 56	7 ■ وَمَا خَلَقْتُ الْجِنَّ وَالْإِنْسَ إِلَّا لِيَعْبُدُونِ
And if they had been patient until you come out to them...	8 وَلَوْ أَنَّهُمْ صَبَرُوا حَتَّى تَخْرُجَ إِلَيْهِمْ
it would certainly have been better for them. 49: 5	9 لَكَانَ خَيْراً لَهُمْ
So that we may glorify You much and remember You much. 20: 34	10 كَيْ نُسَبِّحَكَ كَثِيراً وَنَذْكُرَكَ كَثِيراً
And indeed, we will not enter it until they go out from it. 5: 22	11 وَإِنَّا لَنْ نَدْخُلَهَا حَتَّى يَخْرُجُوا مِنْهَا
Your relatives will not benefit you, nor will your children on the Day of Resurrection. 60: 3	12 لَنْ تَنْفَعَكُمْ أَرْحَامُكُمْ وَلَا أَوْلَادُكُمْ يَوْمَ الْقِيَامَةِ
And they say: He shall not enter Paradise except whoever has been a Jew or a Christian. 2: 111	13 وَقَالُوا لَنْ يَدْخُلَ الْجَنَّةَ إِلَّا مَنْ كَانَ هُوداً أَوْ نَصْرَى
Does he think that noone shall have power over him? 90: 5	14 ■ أَيَحْسَبُ أَنْ لَنْ يَقْدِرَ عَلَيْهِ أَحَدٌ
And what is wrong with you that you do not spend in the way of God. 57: 10	15 ■ وَمَا لَكُمْ أَلَّا تُنْفِقُوا فِي سَبِيلِ اللَّهِ

Notes for text above

■ *Line 1:* أَنْ نَأْكُلَ literally means 'that we should eat'; it is translated simply as 'to eat'. A similar use of the subjunctive is in line 2 and line 3.

■ *Line 7:* The final ن in لِيَعْبُدُونِ is short for the attached pronoun نِي - Me. The alif at the end of

the 3.m.p. subjunctive is dropped after the waw because of the attached pronoun.

■ *Line 14:* Lit. 'that anyone shall not have power over him'.

■ *Line 15:* تُنْفِقُوا is present subjunctive of the Form IV verb - (see Unit 32).

The Jussive mood (مَجْزُوم) of the present tense verb is formed from the indicative as follows:

  i. The forms which end with the final root letter lose their final vowel altogether and take a suk**u**n, e.g. يَكْتُبْ

  ii. The other forms are the same as in the subjunctive.

The jussive mood has a basic meaning of expressing a wish or a command beginning with 'may' or 'let' as in 'may he write' or 'let him write'. It has other uses in Arabic:

• making a negative command;
• negating the past tense.

Like the subjunctive, it is preceded by particles or **'controllers'**.

The conjugation of كَتَبَ **in the jussive is as follows**

Plural	Dual	Singular		Controllers
يَكْتُبُوا	يَكْتُبَا	يَكْتُبْ	3.m.	لَمْ
يَكْتُبْنَ	تَكْتُبَا	تَكْتُبْ	3.f.	لاَ
تَكْتُبُوا	تَكْتُبَا	تَكْتُبْ	2.m.	لَ
تَكْتُبْنَ	تَكْتُبَا	تَكْتُبِى	2.f.	فَلْ
		نَكْتُبْ / أَكْتُبْ	1.m.&f.	وَلْ

The Jussive is used for the following:

(1) Expressing a wish or command

The jussive is used to express a wish or a command - see lines 10, 11, and 13 opposite. In such cases, the jussive is sometimes preceded by لَ or by فَلْ (فَ + لَ). It is then translated as 'May he ...' or 'Let him ...'

فَلْيَعْمَلْ عَمَلاً صَالحاً   Let him do righteous work. 18: 110

(2) Prohibition

Cover-up & transparency
'Do not cover up the truth with falsehood nor conceal the truth knowingly.'
For worldly gain, prestige or power over others, people have long been in the business of cover up and dirty tricks. It is sad to see whole so-called civilizations being built on such misrepresentation and distortion. The power of the global media and their ability to 'create' images, give the perpetrators of such distortions a terrible capacity for manipulation. While people should be more vigilant, the perpetrators of such crimes will ultimately be exposed. Transparency will have a new meaning and dimension. All will be revealed.

The second persons of the jussive mood preceded by لاَ express prohibition: See lines 1, 2 3, 4, 5, and 6 opposite.

لاَ تَجْعَلْ   Do not make (singular).

لاَ تَجْعَلُوا   Do not make (plural).

(3) Negation of the past tense.

A common use of the jussive is to negate the past tense. In such cases, the jussive is controlled by the particle لَمْ . See lines 7, 8, 9, 14 and 15 opposite.

لَمْ يَعْلَمْ   He did not know.

Strengthening of the Jussive

The Jussive is frequently strengthened in the Qur'an by adding ـَنَّ to the various endings and is translated into English as 'certainly':

وَ لَيَعْلَمَنَّ اللَّهُ الَّذِينَ صَدَقُوا   And All**a**h shall certainly know those who have been truthful... 29:11

لَتَدْخُلُنَّ الْمَسْجِدَ الْـحَرَامَ   You shall certainly enter the Sacred Mosque...48:27

Do not make with Allah another god (object of worship). 17: 22	١ لَا تَجْعَلْ مَعَ اللَّهِ إِلَـٰهًا ءَاخَرَ
And do not make equals to Allah. 2: 22	٢ وَلَا تَجْعَلُوا لِلَّهِ أَندَادًا
And do not prostrate to the sun nor to the moon. 41: 37	٣ وَلَا تَسْجُدُوا لِلشَّمْسِ وَلَا لِلْقَمَرِ
And (you both) do not approach this tree. 2: 35	٤ وَلَا تَقْرَبَا هَـٰذِهِ الشَّجَرَةَ
Those are the limits of God - so do not approach them. 2: 187	٥ تِلْكَ حُدُودُ اللَّهِ فَلَا تَقْرَبُوهَا
Do not cover up the truth with falsehood. 2: 42	٦ لَا تَلْبِسُوا الْحَقَّ بِالْبَاطِلِ
Did He not make their plan go astray? 105: 2	٧ أَلَمْ يَجْعَلْ كَيْدَهُمْ فِى تَضْلِيلٍ
Did We not make the earth a cradle? 78: 6	٨ ■ أَلَمْ نَجْعَلِ الْأَرْضَ مِهَـٰدًا
Didn't you know that God knows whatever is in heaven and on earth? 22: 70	٩ أَلَمْ تَعْلَمْ أَنَّ اللَّهَ يَعْلَمُ مَا فِى السَّمَاءِ وَالْأَرْضِ
So let the human being consider from what he has been created. 86: 5	١٠ ■ فَلْيَنظُرِ الْإِنسَانُ مِمَّ خُلِقَ
So let them worship the Lord of this house. 106: 3	١١ فَلْيَعْبُدُوا رَبَّ هَـٰذَا الْبَيْتِ
Whoever does an atom's weight of good shall see it. 99: 7	١٢ وَمَن يَعْمَلْ مِثْقَالَ ذَرَّةٍ خَيْرًا يَرَهُ
Let him do righteous work. 18: 110	١٣ فَلْيَعْمَلْ عَمَلًا صَالِحًا
He (Allah) taught the human being what he did not know. 96: 5	١٤ عَلَّمَ الْإِنسَانَ مَا لَمْ يَعْلَمْ
He did not beget and He was not begotten. 112: 3	١٥ ■ لَمْ يَلِدْ وَلَمْ يُولَدْ

■ *Line 8:* The suk_u_n on the ل in نَجْعَل is replaced by a kasrah to provide a link in pronunciation to a following word. This is to ease the flow in reading and reciting.

The same principle is applied to other words or particles normally ending with a suk_u_n, such as the first word in line 10.

■ *Line 10:* مِمَّ is short for مِنْ + مَا - *from what*.

■ *Line 15:* ' He did not beget' means that He was not the father of anyone.

'He was not begotten' means that He was not born to anyone.

يُولَدُ and يَلَدُ (passive) are from the weak verb وَلَدَ / يَلِدُ , *he begat/he begets*.

Unit 25

The imperative

The English word 'imperative' comes from the Latin word 'to command' and corresponds to the Arabic 'Amr'.

Arabic, however, distinguishes between a command (amr), a request (talab) and a supplication (du'a'). The form of the verb for making all three is, however, the same.

a command   أَمْرٌ

a request   طَلَبٌ

a supplication   دُعَاءٌ

The imperative is formed from the second persons of the jussive by

   i. cutting off the prefixed تَ and its vowel;

   ii. if what remains begins with a letter having a sukun, an initial alif is then added.

   iii. The vowel on the alif is a dammah if the next vowel is a dammah.

    The vowel on the alif is a kasrah if the next vowel is a fat-hah or a kasrah.

The endings of the imperative are the same as the endings of the second persons of the jussive. Imperative forms are used for the second persons only.

Jussive	تَغْفِرْ		تـَجْعَلْ		تَدْخُلْ
Imperative	اغْفِرْ	Forgive!	اجْعَلْ	Make!	أُدْخُلْ	Enter!

If after cutting off the prefixed تَ what remains is a letter with a vowel, then no prefixed alif is needed.

Jussive	تـَقُمْ		تَقُلْ		تَكُنْ
Imperative	قُمْ	Stand!	قُلْ	Say!	كُنْ	Be!

If the imperative is connected in pronunciation to a previous letter and vowel, the initial alif (hamzatu-l wasl) of the imperative is ignored in pronunciation.

Imperative	اغْفِرْ	اجْعَلُوا	اُخْرُجْ
Letter + Imperative	وَاغْفِرْ	وَاجْعَلُوا	فَاخْرُجْ

She guarded her chastity
Maryam , the mother of Isa (Jesus) , is one of the most frequently mentioned names in the Qur'an. She - for her faith in God, her virtue and her chastity and the Pharoah's wife - for her faith and her resistance to tyranny, are mentioned in Surah at-Tahrim (surah 66) as exemplars of those who have faith in God. In contrast, the wife of Prophet Nuh and the wife of Prophet Lut are mentioned in the same surah as examples of those who deny the truth, betray the servants of God and join the ranks of sinners.

In line 12, the word مُتَّقِينَ is left untranslated. It is the plural of مُتَّقِى which basically means one who is careful. He is careful of not overstepping the limits set by God, disobeying Him and so causing harm to himself and others. The word muttaqin is variously translated as 'the God-conscious', 'those who fear God', 'the pious ones', 'the righteous ones' or 'the wary ones'. The translation 'the wary ones" comes very close to the basic meaning of muttaqin.

So judge among people with the Truth. 38: 28	فَاحْكُمْ بَيْنَ النَّاسِ بِالْحَقِّ	1
And forgive us, our Sustainer! 60: 5	وَاغْفِرْ لَنَا رَبَّنَا	2
And remember your Sustainer much. 3: 41	وَاذْكُرْ رَبَّكَ كَثِيرًا	3
O Maryam, be devout to your Sustainer,	يَـٰمَرْيَمُ اقْنُتِي لِرَبِّكِ وَاسْجُدِي	4
prostrate and bow with the ones who bow. 3: 43	وَارْكَعِي مَعَ الرَّاكِعِينَ	5
And it would be said, 'Enter (both of you) the fire with the ones who enter. 66: 10	وَقِيلَ ادْخُلَا النَّارَ مَعَ الدَّاخِلِينَ	6
He said, 'O my father! Do what you are commanded.' 37: 102	قَالَ يَا أَبَتِ افْعَلْ مَا تُؤْمَرُ	7 ▪
And do what you (pl.) are commanded. 2: 68	فَافْعَلُوا مَا تُؤْمَرُونَ	8 ▪
And remember God much that you may be successful. 62:10	وَاذْكُرُوا اللَّهَ كَثِيرًا لَعَلَّكُمْ تُفْلِحُونَ	9 ▪
So remember Me (and) I shall remember you...	فَاذْكُرُونِي أَذْكُرْكُمْ	10 ▪
and give thanks to Me and do not be ungrateful to Me. 2: 152	وَاشْكُرُوا لِي وَ لَا تَكْفُرُونِ	11▪
And know that God is with the muttaqin. 9: 36	وَاعْلَمُوا أَنَّ اللَّهَ مَعَ الْمُتَّقِينَ	12
And say, 'Work' and God will see your work. 9: 105	وَقُلِ اعْمَلُوا فَسَيَرَى اللَّهُ عَمَلَكُمْ	13
Bow and prostrate and worship your Sustainer...	ارْكَعُوا وَاسْجُدُوا وَاعْبُدُوا رَبَّكُمْ	14
and do good that you may be successful. 22: 77	وَافْعَلُوا الْخَيْرَ لَعَلَّكُمْ تُفْلِحُونَ	15 ▪

Notes for text above

▪ *Lines 7 & 8*: The word تُؤْمَرُ 'you are commanded' and its plural in line 8 are passive forms of the present tense. See Unit 26 for the passive of the present.

▪ *Line 10*: The word فَاذْكُرُونِي does not have the alif after the waw of the plural (as in line 9) because there is an attached pronoun نِي after it. The second person plural loses its final alif when it has an attached pronoun.

▪ *Line 11*: The final ن in the word تَكْفُرُونِ is short for نِي, meaning 'Me'.

▪ *Lines 9 & 15*: The word تُفْلِحُونَ is a Form IV verb - see Unit 33.

Unit 26

The passive of the present tense

The suffixes of the passive present tense verb are the same as those of the active.

To form the passive of the simple regular verb in the present tense:

i. put a dammah on the prefix letter;

ii. put a sukun on the first foot letter;

iii. put a fat-hah on the second root letter.

The suffixes of the passive present tense verb are the same as those of the active. **Read down.**

Active	يَسْأَلُ	He asks		يَعْرِفُ	He knows
Passive	يُسْأَلُ	He is/shall be asked		يُعْرَفُ	He is/shall be known
Active	يَخْلُقُونَ	They (m.p.) create		تَحْمِلُونَ	You (m.p.) carry
Passive	يُخْلَقُونَ	They are created		تُحْمَلُونَ	You are/shall be carried

You will remember that the present form of the verb is used to express both the present and the future tenses.

Past continuous or habitual action

Line 8 opposite: Here we have an example of the verb كُنْتُم in the past tense being used with another verb تَعْمَلُونَ in the present tense.

This combination of كَانَ + the present tense is used in Arabic to convey the idea of continuous action in the past or habitual action in the past.

كَانُوا يَعْمَلُونَ They were doing. (past continuous)

كَانُوا يَعْمَلُونَ They used to do/they were wont to do. (habitual action)

Which of the favours of your Sustainer will you both deny?

The question in line 3 opposite is repeated 31 times in Surah ar-Rahman. Notice that the attached pronoun in *rabbikuma* and the verb *tukadh-dhibani* are dual. This is so because, according to many commentators, both human beings and jinns are addressed in this repeated question.

So on that day, none shall be questioned about his sin -	فَيَوْمَئِذٍ لَا يُسْئَلُ عَن ذَنبِهِ	1
neither human being nor jinn.	إِنسٌ وَلَا جَانٌّ	2
So which of the favours of your Sustainer will you both deny?	فَبِأَيِّ ءَالَاءِ رَبِّكُمَا تُكَذِّبَانِ	3
The sinners shall be known by their marks...	يُعْرَفُ الْمُجْرِمُونَ بِسِيمَاهُمْ	4 ■
and they shall be seized by the forelocks and the feet. 55: 39-41	وَيُؤْخَذُ بِالنَّوَاصِى وَالْأَقْدَامِ	5
Their testimony shall be written down and they shall be questioned. 43: 19	سَتُكْتَبُ شَهَادَتُهُمْ وَيُسْأَلُونَ	6
So today, no soul shall be wronged at all...	فَالْيَوْمَ لَا تُظْلَمُ نَفْسٌ شَيْئًا	7 ■
and you shall only be recompensed for what you have been doing. 36: 54	وَلَا تُجْزَوْنَ إِلَّا مَا كُنتُمْ تَعْمَلُونَ	8
We shall not be asked about what you do. 34: 25	وَلَا نُسْئَلُ عَمَّا تَعْمَلُونَ	9 ■
You do not wrong and you are not wronged. 2: 279	لَا تَظْلِمُونَ وَلَا تُظْلَمُونَ	10
They do not create a thing, but they, they are created. 16: 20	لَا يَخْلُقُونَ شَيْئًا وَهُمْ يُخْلَقُونَ	11
Whoever fights in the way of God and is killed or is victorious...	وَمَن يُقَاتِلْ فِى سَبِيلِ اللَّهِ فَيُقْتَلْ أَوْ يَغْلِبْ	12 ■
We shall give him a great reward. 4: 74	فَسَوْفَ نُؤْتِيهِ أَجْرًا عَظِيمًا	13 ■
Obey God and the messenger...	وَأَطِيعُوا اللَّهَ وَالرَّسُولَ	14 ■
that you may be blessed. 3: 132	لَعَلَّكُمْ تُرْحَمُونَ	15

Notes for text above

The first five lines are from Surah ar-Rahman, surah 55.

■ **Line 4:** Note that the verb يُعْرَفُ is grammatically singular whereas the subject مُجْرِمُونَ is plural.

■ **Line 7:** The word نَفْسٌ is feminine and so the verb تُظْلَمُ is also feminine.

■ **Line 9:** عَمَّا is a contraction of عَنْ *concerning*, and مَا *what*.

■ **Line 12:** The word يُقَاتِل is the present tense active of a Form III verb. See Unit 32 for Form III verbs.

■ **Line 13:** نُؤْتِيهِ is the present tense active of a Form IV verb.

■ **Line 14:** أَطِيعُوا is the imperative plural of a Form IV verb.

Access to Qur'anic Arabic ◆ **TEXTBOOK**

Because the verb قَالَ occurs very frequently in various forms in the Qur'an, we give below its conjugation in the three modes of the Present: Indicative (مَرْفُوع), Subjunctive (مَنْصُوب) and Jussive (مَجْزُوم). We also give the Imperative.

Imperative
The imperative is formed from the jussive by dropping the prefix تَـ .

Indicative

Plural	Dual	Singular	
يَقُولُونَ	يَقُولَانِ	يَقُولُ	3.m.
يَقُلْنَ	تَقُولَانِ	تَقُولُ	3.f.
تَقُولُونَ	تَقُولَانِ	تَقُولُ	2.m.
تَقُلْنَ	تَقُولَانِ	تَقُولِينَ	2.f.
نَقُولُ	نَقُولُ	أَقُولُ	1.m.&f.

Subjunctive

Controllers

Plural	Dual	Singular		
يَقُولُوا	يَقُولَا	يَقُولَ	3.m.	
يَقُلْنَ	تَقُولَا	تَقُولَ	3.f.	أَنْ
تَقُولُوا	تَقُولَا	تَقُولَ	2.m.	لَنْ
تَقُلْنَ	تَقُولَا	تَقُولِى	2.f.	حَتَّى
نَقُولَ	نَقُولَ	أَقُولَ	1.m.&f.	لِ

etc

Jussive

Controllers

Plural	Dual	Singular		
يَقُولُوا	يَقُولَا	يَقُلْ	3.m.	
يَقُلْنَ	تَقُولَا	تَقُلْ	3.f.	لَمْ
تَقُولُوا	تَقُولَا	تَقُلْ	2.m.	لَا
تَقُلْنَ	تَقُولَا	تَقُولِى	2.f.	فَلَ
نَقُلْ	نَقُلْ	أَقُلْ	1.m.&f.	وَلَ

Imperative

Plural	Dual	Singular	
قُولُوا	قُولَا	قُلْ	2.m.
قُلْنَ	قُولَا	قُولِى	2.f.

Gently
Musa and his brother Harun received the Divine command to go to the powerful tyrant, the Pharoah of Egypt, and invite him to worship God and purify himself. They felt daunted at the task and feared that the Pharoah, known for his temper and arrogance, would tyrannise them.
Still, they were told to go to the Pharoah and speak to him 'gently' (qawlan layyinan - a gentle speech).
Gentle speech in such a situation requires trust in God and total self-control. Gentleness, rather than harshnes and denunciation, is the recommended method for positive change. There is a duty even to tyrants.

The imperative is formed from the Jussive by dropping the prefix تَـ .

On that day, the human being will say: Where is the place to flee? 75: 10	يَقُولُ الْإِنْسَانُ يَوْمَئِذٍ أَيْنَ الْمَفَرُّ	1
I do not say to you: I am an angel. 6: 50	وَلَا أَقُولُ لَكُمْ إِنِّى مَلَكٌ	2
On (that) day, We shall say to the Hell-fire: Are you filled?	يَوْمَ نَقُولُ لِجَهَنَّمَ هَلِ امْتَلَأْتِ	3
...and it will say: Are there more? 50: 30	وَتَقُولُ هَلْ مِنْ مَزِيدٍ	4
Do you say against God what you do not know? 10: 68	أَتَقُولُونَ عَلَى اللَّهِ مَا لَا تَعْلَمُونَ	5
And they were (so) shaken, that the messenger said... 2: 214	وَزُلْزِلُوا حَتَّى يَقُولَ الرَّسُولُ	6
It is greatly hateful in the sight of God that you should say what you do not do. 61: 3	كَبُرَ مَقْتًا عِنْدَ اللَّهِ أَنْ تَقُولُوا مَا لَا تَفْعَلُونَ	7
Did I not say to you that I (alone) know the hidden (reality) of the heavens and the earth? 2: 33	أَلَمْ أَقُلْ لَكُمْ إِنِّى أَعْلَمُ غَيْبَ السَّمَٰوَٰتِ وَالْأَرْضِ	8
So do not say to them (your parents), 'Uff!' 17: 23	فَلَا تَقُلْ لَهُمَا أُفٍّ	9
Believe in God and His messengers and do not say: (God is) three! 4: 171	فَآمِنُوا بِاللَّهِ وَرُسُلِهِ وَلَا تَقُولُوا ثَلَٰثَةٌ	10
So let them be conscious of God and speak truthfully and directly. 4: 9	■ فَلْيَتَّقُوا اللَّهَ وَلْيَقُولُوا قَوْلًا سَدِيدًا	11
Say: He, God, is One. 112: 1	قُلْ هُوَ اللَّهُ أَحَدٌ	12
And say (f.): Indeed I have vowed to the Beneficent God a fast. 19: 26	فَقُولِى إِنِّى نَذَرْتُ لِلرَّحْمَٰنِ صَوْمًا	13
And speak (both of you) to him gently. 20: 40	■ فَقُولَا لَهُ قَوْلًا لَيِّنًا	14
And speak to people kindly. 2: 43	■ وَقُولُوا لِلنَّاسِ حُسْنًا	15

Notes for text above

■ *Line 11:* قَوْلًا سَدِيدًا - This is an example of an 'absolute accusative' (Arabic: maf'ul mutlaq) formed with the verbal noun - قَوْلًا - of the verb in the sentence .This accusative is called in English grammar 'a cognate object' an example of which is the word 'deed' in the sentence 'He did a deed'.

The adjective سَدِيدًا means both forthright and truthful.

■ *Line 14:* قَوْلًا لَيِّنًا - lit. 'a gentle speech' - is another example of an absolute accusative.

■ *Line 15:* حُسْنًا - an example of the accusative being used as an adverb - 'in a good manner'.

Unit 28

The verb: the present tense of كانَ

Because the verb كانَ occurs very frequently in various forms in the Qur'an, we give below its conjugation in the three modes of the Present: Indicative (مَرْفُوع), Subjunctive (مَنْصُوب) and Jussive (مَجْزُوم). We also give the Imperative.

يَكُ ، تَكُ ، أَكُ

These are shortened forms respectively of the Jussive:

يَكُنْ ، تَكُنْ ، أَكُنْ

Indicative

Plural	Dual	Singular	
يَكُونُونَ	يَكُونَانِ	يَكُونُ	3.m.
يَكُنَّ	تَكُونَانِ	تَكُونُ	3.f.
تَكُونُونَ	تَكُونَانِ	تَكُونُ	2.m.
تَكُنَّ	تَكُونَانِ	تَكُونِينَ	2.f.
نَكُونُ	نَكُونُ	أَكُونُ	1.m.f.

Subjunctive

Plural	Dual	Singular		Controllers
يَكُونُوا	يَكُونَا	يَكُونَ	3.m.	أَنْ
يَكُنَّ	تَكُونَا	تَكُونَ	3.f.	لَنْ
تَكُونُوا	تَكُونَا	تَكُونَ	2.m.	حَتَّى
تَكُنَّ	تَكُونَا	تَكُونِي	2.f.	لِ / لِـ كَيْ
نَكُونَ	نَكُونَ	أَكُونَ	1.m.f.	كَيْلَا

Jussive

Plural	Dual	Singular		Controllers
يَكُونُوا	يَكُونَا	يَكُنْ / يَكُ	3.m.	لَمْ
يَكُنَّ	تَكُونَا	تَكُنْ / تَكُ	3.f.	لَا
تَكُونُوا	تَكُونَا	تَكُنْ / تَكُ	2.m.	فَلَـ
تَكُنَّ	تَكُونَا	تَكُونِي / تَكُ	2.f.	وَلَـ
نَكُنْ / نَكُ	نَكُنْ	أَكُنْ / أَكُ	1.m.f.	

Imperative

Plural	Dual	Singular
كُونُوا	كُونَا	كُنْ
كُنَّ	كُونَا	كُونِي

The imperative is formed from the Jussive by dropping the prefix تَـ .

Belief cannot be forced

The question in line 6 implies that it is impossible to force people to be believers in God. Belief has to come from within, through the use of reflection and reason. 'Let there be no coercion in matters of faith (for) the right way now stands out clearly from error' says the well-known verse (2: 256) of the Qur'an. This disposes of the widespread fallacy that Islam offers unbelievers the choice of 'conversion or the sword'.

1	إِذَا قَضَى أَمْرًا فَإِنَّمَا يَقُولُ لَهُ كُنْ فَيَكُونُ	When He decrees a matter, He only says to it, 'Be!' and it is. 3: 47
2	يَوْمَ يَكُونُ النَّاسُ كَالْفَرَاشِ الْمَبْثُوثِ	On (that) day, mankind will be like scattered moths. 101 : 4
3	وَتَكُونُ الْجِبَالُ كَالْعِهْنِ الْمَنْفُوشِ	And the mountains will be like carded wool. 101: 5
4	أَبَى أَنْ يَكُونَ مِنَ السَّاجِدِينَ	He refused to be with the prostrating ones. 15: 31
5	وَأُمِرْتُ أَنْ أَكُونَ مِنَ الْمُؤْمِنِينَ	And I was commanded to be among the believers. 10: 104
6 ■	أَفَأَنْتَ تُكْرِهُ النَّاسَ حَتَّى يَكُونُوا مُؤْمِنِينَ	Would you force people to be (lit. so that they should be) believers? 10.99
7	لَمْ يَكُنْ شَيْئًا مَذْكُورًا	He was not (even) a thing mentioned. 76: 1
8 ■	وَقَدْ خَلَقْتُكَ مِنْ قَبْلُ وَلَمْ تَكُ شَيْئًا	And I did create you before and you were not (even) a thing. 19: 9
9	قَالُوا أَلَمْ نَكُنْ مَعَكُمْ	They said: Were we not with you? 4: 141
10 ■	وَلَمْ أَكُ بَغِيًّا	And I was not immoral. 19: 20
11	وَلَا تَكُونُوا كَالَّذِينَ نَسُوا اللَّهَ	And do not be like those who have forgotten Allah... 59: 19
12	وَكُنْ مِنَ الشَّاكِرِينَ	And be among those who are thankful. 7:144
13 ■	وَلَا تَكُونَنَّ مِنَ الَّذِينَ كَذَّبُوا بِآيَاتِ اللَّه	And do not ever be among those who denied the signs of Allah...
14	فَتَكُونَ مِنَ الْخَاسِرِينَ	lest you be among the losers. 10: 95
15	يَا أَيُّهَا الَّذِينَ آمَنُوا كُونُوا أَنْصَارَ اللَّهِ	O you who have believed! Be helpers of God. 61: 14

Notes for text above

Remember that the predicate of the verb كَانَ is in the accusative - see, for example, lines 6, 7, 8, 10 and 15.

■ *Line 6:* تُكْرِهُ, *you force*, is the present active of a Form IV verb (see Unit 33).

■ *Line 8:* تَكُ is short for تَكُنْ.
■ *Line 10:* أَكُ is short for أَكُنْ.
■ *Line 13:* تَكُونَنَّ has the emphatic ending which in translation is conveyed by the English word 'ever'.

The active participle in Arabic refers both to the action and the doer of the action.

The active participle is treated as a noun which can have the various gender, number and case endings.

The passive participle in Arabic is also treated as a noun.

The Active Participle

In the English sentence, 'He is writing' - the word 'writing' is known as the active participle of the verb 'to write'. The active participle in English ends in '-ing'.

In Arabic the active participle of a simple three-root (Form I) verb like كَتَبَ is of the pattern كَاتِبٌ. An alif is added to the first root letter; the second root letter takes a kasrah.

The active participle in Arabic refers both to the action and the doer of the action. Thus:

Meaning	Active Participle	Verb
writing, a writer	كَاتِبٌ	كَتَبَ
worshipping, a worshipper	عَابِدٌ	عَبَدَ
disbelieving, a disbeliever	كَافِرٌ	كَفَرَ

With the adding of the ta' marbutah, the active participle becomes feminine. The active participle often takes the sound plural endings:

Plural (acc. & gen.)	Plural (nom.)	Singular	
عَابِدِينَ	عَابِدُونَ	عَابِدٌ	m.
عَابِدَاتٍ	عَابِدَاتٌ	عَابِدَةٌ	f.

The plural of active participles can also be the broken plural:

Broken Plural	Sound Plural	Singular
عُلَمَاءُ	عَالِمُونَ	عَالِمٌ
كُفَّارٌ	كَافِرُونَ	كَافِرٌ

The Passive Participle

In the English sentence 'It was written' - the word 'written' is known as the passive participle of the verb 'to write'.

In Arabic, the passive participle of a Form I verb is of the pattern مَفْعُولٌ. Passive participles take the sound plural endings. Examples of passive participles are:

Meaning	Passive Participle	Verb
written	مَكْتُوب	كَتَبَ
witnessed	مَشْهُود	شَهَدَ
known	مَعْلُوم	عَلِمَ

The passive participle is also treated like a noun. With the adding of the ta' marbutah, the passive participle becomes feminine. The passive participle takes the sound plural endings:

	Plural (acc. & gen.)	Plural (nom.)	Singular	
gathered	مَجْمُوعِينَ	مَجْمُوعُونَ	مَجْمُوعٌ	m.
written	مَكْتُوبَاتٍ	مَكْتُوبَاتٌ	مَكْتُوبَةٌ	f.

Argument sustained

A dominating theme of the Qur'an is the reasoned and sustained argument for the Oneness of God, the Creator of all the worlds. The question (line 5) put to disbelievers and sceptics sets out simply and powerfully the case. They can only have three options:
i. Either they were created out of nothing - by 'spontaneous creation', as it were;
ii. Or, they created themselves;
Clearly these two options are to be rejected as impossible. The conclusion - the third option - is clear: the human being, the world and all that is in it owe their existence to a Creator outside themselves.
It is significant that the word used uniquely for the Creator in the Qur'an is al-Khaliq.

	English	Arabic

Our Sustainer! Verily, You are the gatherer of people on a day about which there is no doubt. 3: 7

1 رَبَّنَا إِنَّكَ جَامِعُ النَّاسِ لِيَوْمٍ لَا رَيْبَ فِيهِ

That is a day to which (all) mankind (shall be) gathered and that is a day (that shall be) witnessed. 11: 103

2 ذَٰلِكَ يَوْمٌ مَجْمُوعٌ لَهُ النَّاسُ وَذَٰلِكَ يَوْمٌ مَشْهُودٌ

And behold! Your Lord said to the angels: I (shall be) appointing a khalifah on earth. 2: 30

3 وَإِذْ قَالَ رَبُّكَ لِلْمَلَائِكَةِ إِنِّى جَاعِلٌ فِى الْأَرْضِ خَلِيفَةً

Say: Allah is the Creator of everything. 13: 16

4 قُلِ اللَّهُ خَالِقُ كُلِّ شَىْءٍ

Is it that they were created without anything, or (were) they the creators (of themselves)? 52: 35

5 أَمْ خُلِقُوا مِنْ غَيْرِ شَىْءٍ أَمْ هُمُ الْخَالِقُونَ

There is no god but He, the Knower of the Unseen and the observable. 59: 22

6 لَا إِلَٰهَ إِلَّا هُوَ عَالِمُ الْغَيْبِ وَالشَّهَادَةِ

Indeed, in that are signs for those who know. 30: 22

7 ■ إِنَّ فِى ذَٰلِكَ لَآيَاتٍ لِلْعَالِمِينَ

Among His servants, only those who have knowledge fear God. 35: 28

8 ■ إِنَّمَا يَخْشَى اللَّهَ مِنْ عِبَادِهِ الْعُلَمَاءُ

The first people and the last (will) certainly be gathered... 56: 49- 50

9 إِنَّ الْأَوَّلِينَ وَالْآخِرِينَ لَمَجْمُوعُونَ

The Hajj (is performed in) known months. 2: 197

10 الْحَجُّ أَشْهُرٌ مَعْلُومَاتٌ

And he entered his garden while he (was) being unjust to himself. 18: 35

11 وَدَخَلَ جَنَّتَهُ وَهُوَ ظَالِمٌ لِنَفْسِهِ

And We did not wrong them, but they - they were the wrongdoers. 43: 76

12 وَمَا ظَلَمْنَاهُمْ وَلَٰكِنْ كَانُوا هُمُ الظَّالِمُونَ

And whoever has been killed unjustly, We have given power to his wali. 17:33

13 ■ وَمَنْ قُتِلَ مَظْلُومًا فَقَدْ جَعَلْنَا لِوَلِيِّهِ سُلْطَانًا

In their possessions is a known right (share) for the one who asks and the deprived. 70: 25

14 فِى أَمْوَالِهِمْ حَقٌّ مَعْلُومٌ لِلسَّائِلِ وَالْمَحْرُومِ

Indeed the recitation of the Qur'an at dawn is ever witnessed (by all that is sacred). 17: 78

15 ■ إِنَّ قُرْءَانَ الْفَجْرِ كَانَ مَشْهُودًا

Notes for text above

■ *Line 7:* Distinguish between عَالِمِين *those who know*, and عَالَمِين, *worlds*. A fat-hah or a kasrah can make a really big difference.

■ *Line 8:* إِنَّمَا *only*, applies to الْعُلَمَاءُ which is the subject of the sentence. The fear of God is a quality only of those who have true knowledge.

■ *Line 13:* Waliy may be translated as 'protector' or 'defender of rights'. It is usually taken to refer here to 'next of kin' or the government or ruling authority.

■ *Line 15:* The verb كَانَ has the sense of 'was' and 'continues to be' and so is translated here as 'is ever'.

Apart from active and passive participles (see previous Unit), other words are derived from verbs in Arabic. In this Unit, we shall deal with verbal nouns, nouns of place and time, and nouns of instrument.

Verbal Nouns

In previous Units and in the Word List, we have suggested that a verb should be learnt in its present and past tense. It is customary also to learn the verbal noun as well. This is a good way of increasing your vocabulary. A good Arabic dictionary will list verbal nouns.

Meaning	Verbal Noun	Verb - Present	Verb - Past
going out, exit	خُرُوجٌ	يَخْرُجُ	خَرَجَ
remembrance	ذِكْرٌ	يَذْكُرُ	ذَكَرَ
patience	صَبْرٌ	يَصْبِرُ	صَبَرَ

We can see that the above verbal nouns are on the pattern of فِعْلٌ , فُعُولٌ and فَعْلٌ .

Verbal nouns of other Form I verbs may be on the pattern of فَعَلٌ e.g. بَصَرٌ .

Translation of the verbal noun into English

(i) The verbal noun in Arabic is sometimes translated into English as **an infinitive**, for example:

So (if) they asked you permission **to leave** (lit. for the leaving) 9: 83

فَاسْتَأْذَنُوكَ لِلْخُرُوجِ

(ii) The Arabic verbal noun may also be translated as a clause, for example:

And you have indeed disbelieved after you had professed faith (lit. after your faith) 9: 66

قَدْ كَفَرْتُمْ بَعْدَ إِيمَانِكُمْ

(iii) The verbal noun in the accusative may be qualified by an adjective. This is translated into English as an adverb, for example:

And speak to him gently (lit. and speak to him a gentle speaking).

فَقُولَا لَهُ قَوْلًا لَيِّنًا

Nouns of place and time

From Form I verbs, these occur in three patterns each beginning with the letter mim:

مَفْعَلَةٌ   مَفْعِلٌ   مَفْعَلٌ

The plural of these nouns is on the pattern of مَفَاعِلُ . which does not take tanwin.

Meaning of Singular	Plural	Noun of place	Verb - Past	
place or time of prostration	مَسَاجِدُ	مَسْجِدٌ	سَجَدَ	to prostrate
habitation, dwelling	مَسَاكِنُ	مَسْكَنٌ / ـةٌ	سَكَنَ	to dwell
grave	مَقَابِرُ	مَقْبَرَةٌ	قَبَرَ	to bury

Nouns of instrument

From Form I verbs, these are formed according to the pattern of مِفْعَـال . The plural is on the pattern of mafa'il

Meaning of Singular	Plural	Noun of instrument	Verb - Past	
key	مَفَاتِحُ	مِفْتَاحٌ	فَتَحَ	to open
ladder, step	مَعَارِجُ	مِعْرَاجٌ	عَرَجَ	to ascend

Children of Adam

Human beings are called 'Children of Adam' in the Qur'an. The human race is one species. It is perhaps significant that human beings as a whole, and not just Muslims, are asked to go to a masjid, which literally means both a place and time of prostration.

1	فَاسْتَئْذَنُوكَ لِلْخُرُوجِ فَقُلْ لَنْ تَخْرُجُوا مَعِيَ أَبَداً	And then (if) they were to ask you permission to go forth, say: Never shall you go forth with me. 9: 83
2	قَدْ كَفَرْتُمْ بَعْدَ إِيمَانِكُمْ	You have indeed disbelieved after (you had professed) your faith. 9: 96
3 ■	وَمَنْ يُشْرِكْ بِاللَّهِ فَقَدْ ضَلَّ ضَلَالاً بَعِيداً	Whoever associates (anything) with God, he has indeed gone far astray. 4:116
4 ■	يَـٰأَيُّهَا الَّذِينَ ءَامَنُوا اذْكُرُوا اللَّهَ ذِكْراً كَثِيراً	O you who have believed! Remember God much. 33: 41
5 ■	فَاصْبِرْ صَبْراً جَمِيلاً	So (O believers) endure (adversity) with beautiful endurance. 70: 5
6 ■	وَقُولُوا قَوْلاً سَدِيداً	Be conscious of God and speak truthfully and directly. 33: 70
7 ■	وَيَنْصُرَكَ اللَّهُ نَصْراً عَزِيزاً	And (so that) God might help you (O Muhammad) with powerful help. 48: 3
8 ■	فَمَنْ كَانَ يَرْجُوا لِقَاءَ رَبِّهِ فَلْيَعْمَلْ عَمَلاً صَالِحاً	So whoever expects to meet his Sustainer, then let him act righteously. 18: 110
9 ■	يَابَنِي ءَادَمَ خُذُوا زِينَتَكُمْ عِنْدَ كُلِّ مَسْجِدٍ	O Children of Adam! Take (to) your adornment at every time and place of worship. 7: 31
10	وَمَنْ أَظْلَمُ مِمَّنْ مَنَعَ مَسَاجِدَ اللَّهِ	And who is more wicked than the one who bars the places of worship of God ...
11	أَنْ يُذْكَرَ فِيهَا اسْمُهُ	that His name should be mentioned in them. 2:114
12 ■	لَقَدْ كَانَ لِسَبَأٍ فِي مَسْكَنِهِمْ ءَايَةٌ	Indeed, in their habitation, (the people of) Saba had evidence (of God's grace). 34: 15
13	وَتِلْكَ مَسَاكِنُهُمْ لَمْ تُسْكَنْ مِنْ بَعْدِهِمْ	And those habitations of theirs have not been dwelt in after them... 28: 58
14 ■	أَلْهَاكُمُ التَّكَاثُرُ حَتَّى زُرْتُمُ الْمَقَابِرَ	Competing for ever more wealth distracts you until you visit (reach) the graves. 102: 1-2
15	وَعِنْدَهُ مَفَاتِحُ الْغَيْبِ لَا يَعْلَمُهَا إِلاَّ هُوَ	And with Him are the keys of the Unseen. None knows them but He. 6: 59

Notes for text above

■ **Lines 3, 4, 5, 6, 7 and 8:** The verbal nouns in the accusative are called 'absolute accusatives' - maf'ul mutlaq.

■ **Line 9:** The word مَسْجِد signifies both a place and time of prostration, and not only a mosque.

■ **Line 12:** Notice how كَانَ with the preposition لِ is used to show possession in the past tense.

■ **Line 14:** أَلْهَى is a Form IV verb from لَهَا meaning 'to have a good time, to play, to fritter away, to distract oneself'. The noun from لَهَا is لَهْوٌ meaning 'amusement, diversion, distraction'.

So far we have been dealing mainly with simple, regular Form I verbs. From the basic Form I verb or root, other verb forms are derived by:

    i. doubling a root letter

    ii. lengthening a root letter

    iii. adding other letters either as prefixes or between root letters

    iv. a combination of the above.

Of the nine derived Forms, Forms II, IV and X are used frequently in the Qur'an.

Form II - Past

All Form II verbs in the past tense are formed by doubling the second root letter of the simple Form I verb.

Form I	he knew	عَلِمَ	كَذَبَ	he lied
Form II	he taught	عَلَّمَ	كَذَّبَ	he denied

The suffixes of a Form II verb in the past in its singular, dual and plural forms are the same as for a Form I verb in the past. Indeed, the suffixes for all verb Forms in the past tense are the same. For example:

Form I	you (m.s.) knew	عَلِمْتَ	كَذَبْتُمْ	you (m.p.) lied
Form II	you (m.s.) taught	عَلَّمْتَ	كَذَّبْتُمْ	you (m.p.) denied

Form II - Present

The Present of all Form II verbs follows the same pattern:

    i. The vowel on the first prefixed letter has a dammah;

    ii. The vowel with the second root letter is a kasrah in the present active.

    iii. The vowel with the second root letter is a fat-hah in the present passive.

The suffixes are the same as for a Form I verb in the present. Indeed the suffixes for all verb Forms I - X are the same in the present.

Past Active	he taught	عَلَّمَ	نَزَّلَ	he sent down
Present Active	he teaches	يُعَلِّمُ	يُنَزِّلُ	he sends down
Present Passive	he is taught	يُعَلَّمُ	يُنَزَّلُ	it is sent down
Imperative	teach!	عَلِّمْ	نَزِّلْ	send down!

It is important to know the following forms as well because this will show how words are built up. Remember that in Arabic the active participle denotes the action as well as the person performing the action.

Active participle	teaching, teacher	مُعَلِّم	مُنَزِّلُ	one who sends down
Passive participle	taught	مُعَلَّم	مُنَزَّلُ	sent down
Verbal noun	a teaching, instruction	تَعْلِيم	تَنْزِيل	a sending down, revelation

Meaning patterns

A Form II verb may denote

(i) causation:

عَلِمَ means 'he knew';

عَلَّمَ means "he caused s.o. to know", i.e. 'he taught'.

نَزَلَ means 'he descended'

نَزَّلَ means 'he caused to descend', i.e. 'he sent down' or 'he revealed'.

(ii) intensity of action:

قَتَلَ means 'he killed

قَتَّلَ means 'he massacred'.

(iii) estimation:

صَدَقَ means 'he spoke the truth'

صَدَّقَ means 'he considered s.o. truthful' i.e. - 'he believed'.

In addition to the Form I verb, there are nine Derived Forms used. For all these, Roman numerals from I - X are used. Each Form follows its own pattern for the past tense and a set pattern for the present. It is important to get used to recognizing these patterns. This will be a great help in building up a vocabulary and in reading correctly.

Three main roles

As a witness, a bringer of good news and a warner - these are three main roles which the noble Prophet Muhammad, may God bless him and grant him peace, was sent by God to fulfil (line 13 opposite).
A witness - that God is One and nothing is worthy of worship besides Him.
A bringer of good news - the good news of God's pleasure and rewards - of Paradise - for all who believe and do good works.
A warner - of pain and chastisement for those who refuse to acknowledge their Creator and who persist in wrong-doing.
These have been and are the three main roles of all callers to Truth.

He created the human being. He taught him clear speech. 55: 4	خَلَقَ الْإِنْسَانَ عَلَّمَهُ الْبَيَانَ ١
He taught the human being what he did not know. 96: 5	عَلَّمَ الْإِنْسَانَ مَا لَمْ يَعْلَمْ ٢
They said: Glory be to You! No knowledge have we except what You have taught us. 2: 32	قَالُوا سُبْحَانَكَ لَا عِلْمَ لَنَا إِلَّا مَا عَلَّمْتَنَا ٣
And He teaches him the Book and the Wisdom and purifies him. 2: 129	وَيُعَلِّمُهُ الْكِتَابَ وَالْحِكْمَةَ وَيُزَكِّيهِ ٤
But the satans have disbelieved, teaching people sorcery. 2: 102	وَلَكِنَّ الشَّيَاطِينَ كَفَرُوا يُعَلِّمُونَ النَّاسَ السِّحْرَ ٥
We have made the messages clear for you that you may use your reason. 57: 17	قَدْ بَيَّنَّا لَكُمُ الْآيَاتِ لَعَلَّكُمْ تَعْقِلُونَ ٦ ■
Thus does Allah make clear His messages to you that you may use your reason. 2: 247	كَذَٰلِكَ يُبَيِّنُ اللَّهُ لَكُمُ الْآيَاتِ لَعَلَّكُمْ تَعْقِلُونَ ٧
Whatever is in the heavens and earth glorifies Allah. 57: 1	سَبَّحَ لِلَّهِ مَا فِي السَّمَاوَاتِ وَالْأَرْضِ ٨
Whatever is in the heavens and earth glorifies Him. 24: 41	يُسَبِّحُ لَهُ مَا فِي السَّمَاوَاتِ وَالْأَرْضِ ٩
Glorify the name of your Sustainer, the Most High. 87: 1	سَبِّحِ اسْمَ رَبِّكَ الْأَعْلَى ١٠ ■
And he said, O people! We have been taught the speech of birds. 27: 16	وَقَالَ يَا أَيُّهَا النَّاسُ عُلِّمْنَا مَنْطِقَ الطَّيْرِ ١١ ■
(They do not like) that it should be revealed to you (anything) of good from your Lord. 2: 105	أَنْ يُنَزَّلَ عَلَيْكُمْ مِنْ خَيْرٍ مِنْ رَبِّكُمْ ١٢
O Prophet! Indeed We have sent you as a witness, a bringer of good news and a warner. 33: 45	يَا أَيُّهَا النَّبِيُّ إِنَّا أَرْسَلْنَاكَ شَاهِدًا وَمُبَشِّرًا وَنَذِيرًا ١٣ ■
Then they turned away from him and said, 'A taught person, insane.' 44: 14	ثُمَّ تَوَلَّوْا عَنْهُ وَقَالُوا مُعَلَّمٌ مَجْنُونٌ ١٤
And recite the Qur'an in a measured recitation. 73: 4	وَرَتِّلِ الْقُرْءَانَ تَرْتِيلًا ١٥

Notes for text above

■ *Line 6:* بَيَّنَّا is a contraction of بَيَّنْنَا - 'We have made clear'.

■ *Line 10:* A kasrah replaces the sukun on the last letter in سَبِّحِ - Glorify!'. See also رَتِّلِ in line 15.

■ *Line 11:* عُلِّمْنَا is passive. This is shown by the dammah on the first letter.

■ *Line 13:* مُبَشِّرًا is the active participle of بَشَّرَ. The accusative here denotes 'as a bringer of good news'.

نَذِيرًا and مُبَشِّرًا , شَاهِدًا are hal constructions and therefore accusative. (see Unit 37).

Unit 32

Derived Forms of the Verb - Form III

Meaning Patterns
A Form III verb may denote
(i) the doing of an action to someone
(ii) the attempt to do something to someone.

As mentioned in the last Unit, each Derived Form of the Verb follows its own set pattern for the past tense and a set pattern for the present. It is important to get used to recognizing these patterns. This will be a great help in building up a vocabulary and reading correctly.

Form III - Past

All Form III verbs in the past tense are formed by adding an alif after the first root letter of the simple Form I verb.

Form I	he preceded	سَبَقَ	قَتَلَ	he killed
Form III	he competed with	سَابَقَ	قَاتَلَ	he fought

The suffixes for all verb Forms in the past tense are the same. For example:

Form I	I wrote	كَتَبْتُ	قَتَلُوا	they (m.p.) killed
Form III	I corresponded	كَاتَبْتُ	قَاتَلُوا	they (m.p.) fought

Form III- Present

Form III verbs in the present have the same following features as Form II present tense verbs:

    i. the vowel on the first prefixed letter has a dammah;
    ii. the vowel with the second root letter is a kasrah in the present active;
    iii. the vowel with the second root letter is a fat-hah in the present passive.

The suffixes are the same as for a Form I verb in the present. Indeed the suffixes for all verb Forms I - X are the same in the present.

Past Active	he competed	سَابَقَ	قَاتَلَ	he fought
Present Active	he competes	يُسَابِقُ	يُقَاتِلُ	he fights
Present Passive			يُقَاتَلُ	he is fought
Imperative	compete	سَابِقْ	قَاتِلْ	Fight! (s)

It is important to know the following forms as well because this will show how words are built up:

Active participle	competing,	مُسَابِق	مُقَاتِل	fighting, a warrior
Passive participle	competed	مُسَابَق	مُقَاتَل	fought
Verbal noun	competition	مُسَابَقَة	قِتَال	fighting

The verbal noun of a Form III verb may be patterned either on مُفَاعَلَة as in مُسَابَقَة or on فِعَال as in قِتَال.

Meaning Patterns

A Form III verb may denote

    (i) the doing of an action to someone, e.g.

    كَاتَبَ he wrote to, corresponded with - from كَتَبَ he wrote.

    قَاوَمَ he stood up, he resisted - from قَامَ he stood.

    (ii) the attempt to do something to someone, e.g.

    قَاتَلَ he tried to kill, he fought with - from قَتَلَ, he killed.

    سَابَقَ he competed with - from سَبَقَ, he preceded.

By council and consent
The command to consult (line 9 opposite) is addressed in the first instance to the noble Prophet and, after him, to all who are in charge of Muslim affairs.
The attached pronoun *hum* refers to the believers, - that is, the whole Muslim community.
The word *al-amr* - literally, *the matter* - refers to affairs of public concern.
This verse lays down a basic feature of Muslim government - that it is by consultation and consent. There are two views regarding the decision reached after such consultation or *shura*: that the ruler is either free to accept or reject it. The Prophet considered himself bound by the decision of his *shura*.

1 ■ وَمَنْ جَاهَدَ فَإِنَّمَا يُجَاهِدُ لِنَفْسِهِ

And whoever strives, he strives for his own self. 9: 19

2 ■ وَلَا تُطِعِ الْكَـٰفِرِينَ وَجَاهِدْهُم بِهِ جِهَادًا كَبِيرًا

And do not obey the disbelievers, and strive with them with a great striving. 25: 52

3 ■ حَافِظُوا عَلَى الصَّلَوَاتِ وَالصَّلَوٰةِ الْوُسْطَىٰ

Maintain the Salats, and the middle Salat. 2: 238

4 ■ وَقَاتَلُوا وَقُتِلُوا

And they fought and were killed. 3: 195

5 ■ وَمَا لَكُمْ لَا تُقَاتِلُونَ فِى سَبِيلِ اللَّهِ

What is wrong with you - you do not fight in the way of God? 4: 75

6 ■ وَالَّذِينَ ءَامَنُوا وَهَاجَرُوا وَجَاهَدُوا فِى سَبِيلِ اللَّهِ

And those who believed and migrated and strove in the way of God... 8: 74

7 ■ إِنَّ اللَّهَ يُحِبُّ الَّذِينَ يُقَاتِلُونَ فِى سَبِيلِ اللَّهِ صَفًّا

Indeed, God loves those who fight in the way of God, in ranks. 61: 4

8 ■ وَشَارِكْهُمْ فِى الْأَمْوَالِ وَالْأَوْلَادِ

And share with them in possessions and children. 17: 64

9 ■ وَشَاوِرْهُمْ فِى الْأَمْرِ

And consult them in the matter. 3: 159

10 ■ فَاذْهَبْ أَنتَ وَرَبُّكَ فَقَاتِلَا إِنَّا هَـٰهُنَا قَاعِدُونَ

Go, you and your Lord, and fight! We shall be sitting here. 5: 24

11 ■ كُتِبَ عَلَيْكُمُ الْقِتَالُ وَهُوَ كُرْهٌ لَكُمْ

Fighting has been prescribed for you while it may be detestable to you. 2 216

12 ■ أُذِنَ لِلَّذِينَ يُقَاتَلُونَ بِأَنَّهُمْ ظُلِمُوا

Permission (to fight) has been given to those who are fought against because they have been wronged. 22: 39

13 ■ لَقَدْ رَضِيَ اللَّهُ عَنِ الْمُؤْمِنِينَ إِذْ يُبَايِعُونَكَ تَحْتَ الشَّجَرَةِ

God is pleased with the believers when they pledge allegiance to you under the tree. 48: 18

14 ■ إِذَا جَاءَتِ الْمُؤْمِنَاتُ يُبَايِعْنَكَ

When the believing women come to you, let them pledge allegiance to you

عَلَى أَنْ لَا يُشْرِكْنَ بِاللَّهِ شَيْئًا

on the basis that they will not associate anything with God. 60: 12

15 ■ إِنَّ الَّذِينَ يُبَايِعُونَكَ إِنَّمَا يُبَايِعُونَ اللَّهَ

Indeed those who pledge allegiance to you, they are only pledging allegiance to God. 48: 10

Notes for text above

صَفٌّ / صُفُوفٌ   row, rank/ pl.

قَعَدَ / يَقْعُدُ   to sit

كَرِهَ / يَكْرَهُ   to dislike, hate

كُرْهٌ   detestation

بَايَعَ / يُبَايِعُ   to pledge allegiance

■ **Line 1:** جَاهَدَ is past tense, but preceded here by مَنْ it is translated as the present.

Line 3: الصَّلَوٰةِ الْوُسْطَىٰ , the Middle Prayer, is said to refer either to to Salat al-'Asr or to Salat al-Fajr. وُسْطَىٰ is the feminine form of the comparative adjective. It is on the pattern of كُبْرَىٰ.

■ **Line 5:** مَا لَكُمْ - 'What's the matter with you?'

■ **Line 10:** قَاتِلَا is dual and imperative.

Unit 33

Derived Forms of the Verb - Form IV

This is one of the most common of the derived forms used in the Qur'an.

Form IV - Past

All Form IV verbs in the past tense are formed by placing a sukun on the first root letter of the verb and prefixing this by an alif with a hamzatu-l qat' and a fat-hah.

Form I	he entered	دَخَلَ	نَزَلَ	he descended
Form IV	he admitted	أَدْخَلَ	أَنْزَلَ	he sent down, revealed

The suffixes of a Form IV verb in the past in its singular, dual and plural forms are the same as for a Form I verb in the past. Indeed, the suffixes for all verb Forms in the past tense are the same. For example:

Form I	he (m.s.) left	خَرَجَ	نَزَلْنَا	We descended
Form IV	he (m.s.) expelled	أَخْرَجَ	أَنْزَلْنَا	We sent down, revealed

The word خَرَجَ may also mean 'he came out'.

The word أَخْرَجَ may also mean 'he brought out', 'he produced'. Exact meanings can only be determined by the context.

Form IV - Present

The Present of all Form IV verbs follows the same pattern:
   i. the vowel on the first prefixed letter has a dammah;
   ii. the vowel with the second root letter is a kasrah in the present active;
   iii. the vowel with the second root letter is a fat-hah in the present passive.

The suffixes are the same as for a Form I verb in the present.

Past Active	he expelled	أَخْرَجَ	أَنْزَلَ	he sent down
Present Active	he expels	يُخْرِجُ	يُنْزِلُ	he sends down
Present Passive	he is expelled	يُخْرَجُ	يُنْزَلُ	it is sent down
Imperative	expel!	أَخْرِجْ	أَنْزِلْ	send down!

It is important to know the following forms as well because this will show how words are built up:

Active participle	expelling, expeller	مُخْرِج	مُنْزِل	one who sends down
Passive participle	expelled	مُخْرَج	مُنْزَل	sent down
Verbal noun	expulsion	إِخْرَاج	إِنْزَال	a sending down, revelation

---

The Form IV verb is one

of the most common of the derived forms used in the Qur'an.

Meaning Pattern
Form IV verbs are generally causative in relation to the Form I verb, e.g:
Form I - to enter
Form IV - to cause someone to enter, to admit.

We are only setting things right!

Those who cause disorder, ruin and corruption on earth often portray themselves as the salt of the earth, the saviours of mankind, bringers of peace, progress and prosperity. Verse 11 of Surah al-Baqarah (lines 11 & 12 opposite) may well be applied to much of contemporary 'civilization' as we know it. We need to look at the reality beyond the rhetoric.

Meaning Patterns

A Form IV verb is generally causative.

أَدْخَلَ to cause to enter i.e. to admit - from دَخَلَ, to enter

أَنْزَلَ to cause to descend i.e. to send down or reveal - from نَزَلَ, to descend

أَطْعَمَ to cause to eat i.e. to feed - from طَعَمَ, to taste, to eat.

He sent His messenger with the guidance and the religion of Truth. 9: 93	١ أَرْسَلَ رَسُولَهُ بِالْهُدَى وَدِينِ الْحَقِّ
We have not sent you (O Muhammad) except as a mercy to all the worlds. 21: 107	٢ وَمَا أَرْسَلْنَاكَ إِلاَّ رَحْمَةً لِلْعَالَمِينَ
Behold! His Sustainer said to him, Submit! 2: 131	٣ إِذْ قَالَ لَهُ رَبُّهُ أَسْلِمْ
He said: I have submitted to the Sustainer of the worlds. 2: 131	٤ قَالَ أَسْلَمْتُ لِرَبِّ الْعَالَمِينَ
They said: Indeed we have been sent to a sinful people. 15: 58	٥ قَالُوا إِنَّا أُرْسِلْنَا إِلَى قَوْمٍ مُجْرِمِينَ
God shall admit them into His mercy. 9: 99	٦ سَيُدْخِلُهُمُ اللَّهُ فِى رَحْمَتِهِ
Those who have disbelieved, it is the same to them whether you warned them...	٧ ■ إِنَّ الَّذِينَ كَفَرُوا سَوَاءٌ عَلَيْهِمْ ءَأَنْذَرْتَهُمْ
or did not warn them - they will not believe. 2: 6	٨ ■ أَمْ لَمْ تُنْذِرْهُمْ لاَ يُؤْمِنُونَ
The nomad Arabs have said, We have believed. Say, you have not believed ...	٩ ■ قَالَتِ الْأَعْرَابُ ءَامَنَّا قُلْ لَمْ تُؤْمِنُوا
but say (instead), We have submitted. 49: 14	١٠ ■ وَلَكِنْ قُولُوا أَسْلَمْنَا
And when it is said to them, Do not make corruption on earth ...	١١ ■ وَإِذَا قِيلَ لَهُمْ لاَ تُفْسِدُوا فِى الْأَرْضِ
they say, We are only reformers. 2: 11	١٢ قَالُوا إِنَّمَا نَحْنُ مُصْلِحُونَ
And they were amazed that a warner came to them from among them. 34: 4	١٣ وَعَجِبُوا أَنْ جَاءَهُمْ مُنْذِرٌ مِنْهُمْ
Indeed We, We have been the senders. 44: 5	١٤ ■ إِنَّا كُنَّا مُرْسِلِينَ
They said: Our Sustainer knows that we have indeed been sent to you. 36: 16	١٥ ■ قَالُوا رَبُّنَا يَعْلَمُ إِنَّا إِلَيْكُمْ لَمُرْسَلُونَ

Notes for text above

■ *Lines 7 & 8:* أ followed by أَمْ means 'whether ... or'.

■ *Lines 9 & 10:* A distinction is made here between ءَامَنَ *to believe*, and أَسْلَمَ, *to submit*. Submission which is the meaning of the word 'islam' (the verbal noun of أَسْلَمَ) can merely be an outward or superficial acceptance of the truth. 'Iman' (the verbal noun from ءَامَنَ) which means *faith*, implies something which comes from within, something that is deep and lasting.

■ *Lines 14 & 15:* Notice the major difference in meaning between مُرْسِلِينَ and مُرْسَلِينَ caused by the difference of a single vowel.

The formation and conjugation of verb Forms V and VI have some similarities. For example, the past tense of both begin with ـَتـ. There is also a string of fat-hahs in the past and in the present forms.

Form V - Past
All Form V verbs in the past tense are formed by prefixing a ـَتـ to the Form II verb.
The suffixes of a Form V verb in the past are the same as for all past tense verbs.

Form II	he taught	عَلَّمَ	نَزَّلَ	he sent down
Form V	he learnt	تَعَلَّمَ	تَنَزَّلَ	he descended

Forms V - Present
The Present of all Form V verbs have the same prefixes as a Form I verb.
The suffixes are the same as for a Form I verb in the present. Notice the string of vowel a's in the present.

Past Active	he depended	تَوَكَّلَ	تَعَلَّمَ	he learnt
Present active	he depends	يَتَوَكَّلُ	يَتَعَلَّمُ	he learns
Active participle	depending	مُتَوَكِّل	مُتَعَلِّم	a learning person
Passive participle	dependent	مُتَوَكَّل		
Verbal Noun	dependance	تَوَكُّل	تَعَلُّم	learning

Form VI - Past
Form VI verbs often have the sense of reciprocity - that is, of doing something with others.
All Form VI verbs in the past tense are formed by prefixing a ـَتـ to the Form III verb.
The suffixes of a Form VI verb in the past are the same as for all past tense verbs.

Form III	he disputed with you	نَازَعَكَ	قَاتَلَهُ	he fought with him
Form VI	they disputed among themselves	تَنَازَعُوا	تَقَاتَلَ القَوْمُ	the people fought each other

Forms VI - Present
The Present of all Form VI verbs have the same prefixes as a Form I verb.
The suffixes are the same as for a Form I verb in the present. Notice the string of vowel a's in the present.

Present active	they dispute among themselves	يَتَنَازَعُونَ	يَتَعَارَفُونَ	they know one another
Verbal noun	mutual disputation	تَنَازُع	تَعَارُف	knowing one another

نَزَعَ / يَنْزِعُ	I. to withdraw	قُرْبَان	offering
نَازَعَ / يُنَازِعُ	III. to dispute with s.o.	طَبَعَ / يَطْبَعُ	he sealed/ he seals
تَنَازَعَ / يَتَنَازَعُ	VI. to dispute with one another	تَدَايَنَ	VI. to give or take credit
تَقَبَّلَ / يَتَقَبَّلُ	he accepted/he accepts	قُبُول	acceptance

Knowing One Another

This is the title of a book on anthropology inspired by verse 13 of Surah al-Hujurat much of which deals with the basis of human relationships and of dealing with various types of divisions and conflicts in human situations. The verse demolishes any notion of ethnic or racial superiority and lays down firmly the principle that the most honourable in the sight of God are those who are most deeply conscious of Him.

So her Sustainer accepted her with goodly acceptance. 3: 37	1	فَتَقَبَّلَهَا رَبُّهَا بِقُبُولٍ حَسَنٍ
God only accepts from the muttaqin. 5: 27	2	إِنَّمَا يَتَقَبَّلُ اللَّهُ مِنَ الْمُتَّقِينَ
Our Sustainer! Accept from us. Indeed, You are the Hearer, the Knower. 2: 127	3	رَبَّنَا تَقَبَّلْ مِنَّا إِنَّكَ أَنْتَ السَّمِيعُ الْعَلِيمُ
Our Sustainer, and accept my supplication.14: 40	4 ■	رَبَّنَا وَتَقَبَّلْ دُعَاء
When they both approached with an offering, it was accepted from one of them...	5	إِذْ قَرَّبَا قُرْبَانًا فَتُقُبِّلَ مِنْ أَحَدِهِمَا
and it was not accepted from the other. 5: 27	6	وَلَمْ يَتَقَبَّلْ مِنَ الْأَخَرِ
(Thus) does God seal the heart of every arrogant, tyrannical person. 40: 35	7 ■	يَطْبَعُ اللَّهُ عَلَى كُلِّ قَلْبِ مُتَكَبِّرٍ جَبَّارٍ
Is not the abode of the arrogant ones in hell? 39: 60	8	أَلَيْسَ فِي جَهَنَّمَ مَثْوًى لِلْمُتَكَبِّرِينَ
The angels shall descend on them. 41: 30	9	تَتَنَزَّلُ عَلَيْهِمُ الْمَلَائِكَةُ
Whenever you give or take credit for a stated term, write it down. 2: 282	10 ■	إِذَا تَدَايَنْتُمْ بِدَيْنٍ إِلَى أَجَلٍ مُسَمًّى فَاكْتُبُوهُ
About what do they ask one another - about the awesome news. 78: 1	11	عَمَّ يَتَسَاءَلُونَ ، عَنِ النَّبَإِ الْعَظِيمِ
And We made you into nations and tribes so that you may know one another. 49: 13	12	وَجَعَلْنَاكُمْ شُعُوبًا وَقَبَائِلَ لِتَعَارَفُوا
And help one another to righteousness and taqwa...	13 ■	وَتَعَاوَنُوا عَلَى الْبِرِّ وَالتَّقْوَى
and do not help one another to sin and transgression. 5: 2	14	وَلَا تَعَاوَنُوا عَلَى الْإِثْمِ وَالْعُدْوَانِ
And encourage one another in the truth, and encourage one another in patience. 103: 3	15	وَتَوَاصَوْا بِالْحَقِّ وَتَوَاصَوْا بِالصَّبْرِ

Notes for text above

■ *Line 4:* دُعَاء is short for دُعَاءِي, *my supplication.*

■ *Lines 7:* مُتَكَبِّر, *one who is arrogant*, is the active participle of تَكَبَّر, *he considered himself great* - i.e. *he was arrogant.* مُتَكَبِّرِين (line 8) is the active participle plural, genitive.

■ *Lines 10:* تَدَايَنْتُمْ implies both incurring a debt on

the one hand and giving credit on the other - i.e. *giving and receiving credit from one another* - from the word دَيْن , *a debt.*

■ *Line 13:* The words نَسْتَعِين and تَعَاوَنُوا (Form X - see Unit 36) come from the same root word, the verbal noun of which is عَوْن , *help.*

Hamzatu-l wasl

means 'a connecting hamzah'. Its sign is a small ṣad placed above the alif.
Ignore the alif with hamzatu-l wasl when it is preceded by a vowel: which is pronounced

وَٱنطَلَقَ

and he set forth.

These three verb Forms in the past begin with an alif having a kasrah. The alif takes a hamzatu-l wasl.

Form VII Past & Present

This Form does not occur frequently in the Qur'an. It is the passive or reflexive of the Form I verb. It cannot take a direct object.
The past tense is formed by placing the prefix اِنْ before the Form I verb.
The present is formed by using the same prefixes as a Form I verb followed by a nun with a sukun. The second root letter then takes a kasrah.

	Present	Past	
he turns	يَنقَلِبُ	اِنقَلَبَ	he turned
he sets forth	يَنطَلِقُ	اِنطَلَقَ	he set forth

Examples of active and passive participles and verbal nouns of Form VII:

Active participle	splitting	مُنفَطِر	مُنقَلِب	turning; one who turns
Passive participle	split	مُنفَطَر	مُنقَلَب	overturned
Verbal noun	a splitting	اِنفِطَار	اِنقِلَاب	overturning, a revolution

Form VIII - Past

A Form VIII verb is made by placing a sukun on the first root letter and prefixing this with an alif with a kasrah.
A ت is then inserted between the first and second root letters.

he followed	تَبِعَ	سَمِعَ	he heard
he followed VIII	اِتَّبَعَ	اِستَمَعَ	he listened VIII

Form VIII - Present

The form VIII verb in the present have the following features:
   i. The vowel on the first prefixed letter has a fat-hah;
   ii. The vowel with the second root letter is a kasrah in the present active.
   iii. The vowel with the second root letter is a fat-hah in the present passive.
The suffixes are the same as for a Form I verb in the present.

Past Active	he followed	اِتَّبَعَ	اِستَمَعَ	he listened
Present Active	he follows	يَتَّبِعُ	يَستَمِعُ	he listens
Imperative	Follow!	اِتَّبِع	اِستَمِع	Listen!

Examples of active and passive participles and verbal nouns of Form VIII

Active participle	following; a follower	مُتَّبِع	مُستَمِع	listening; a listener
Passive participle	followed	مُتَّبَع	مُستَمَع	listened
Verbal Noun	following	اِتِّبَاع	اِستِمَاع	listening

The verbal noun of a Form VIII verb is patterned on اِفتِعَال .
Meaning Patterns: Form VIII is usually the reflexive of the Form I verb.

'Reflexive' implies to do something for oneself. For example, أَخَذَ (Form I) means 'he took'. اِتَّخَذَ (Form VIII) meanis 'he took for himself', or 'he adopted'.

Sometimes the Ist and VIIIth forms occur without much difference in meanings:
شَرَى/يَشرِى he bought, he buys اِشتَرَى/يَشتَرِى he bought, he buys.

هَوَاء

The god of caprice, whims and desires

The word *hawa'* is used in both lines 8 and 13 opposite. It signifies whims, caprice, selfish desires and passions. When a person follows his own hawa' as opposed to the wise and just guidance of the Wise and Just Creator, he becomes a slave to his hawa' and this in effect becomes his god or object of obedience and worship. The result of this short-sighted arrogance is ruin.
The reference to hawa' in line 13 is a pointer to the fact that caprice and arbitrariness is not a hallmark of good Islamic judgement which is based on firm principles and values.

And the chiefs among them set off... 38: 6	وَانْطَلَقَ الْمَلَأُ مِنْهُمْ ١
So they both set off until (after) they had sailed on the boat - he bore a hole in it. 18: 71	فَانْطَلَقَا حَتَّى إِذَا رَكِبَا فِى السَّفِينَةِ خَرَقَهَا ٢
Then they turned away; God has turned their hearts away (from the truth). 9: 127	ثُمَّ انْصَرَفُوا ، صَرَفَ اللَّهُ قُلُوبَهُمْ ٣
When the sky is split asunder and when the planets are scattered... 82: 1	إِذَا السَّمَاءُ انْفَطَرَتْ ، وَإِذَا الْكَوَاكِبُ انْتَثَرَتْ ٤
They said, To our Sustainer, we are turning. 7: 125	قَالُوا إِنَّا إِلَى رَبِّنَا مُنْقَلِبُونَ ٥
... a company of jinn listened... 72: 1	اسْتَمَعَ نَفَرٌ مِنَ الْجِنِّ ٦
Peace be on whoever follows the guidance. 20: 47	وَالسَّلَامُ عَلَى مَنِ اتَّبَعَ الْهُدَى ٧
Have you seen the one who has taken his desire as his god? 25: 43	■ أَرَأَيْتَ مَنِ اتَّخَذَ إِلَـهَهُ هَوَاهُ ٨
You have taken the signs of God as a joke. 45: 35	■ اتَّخَذْتُمْ ءَايَاتِ اللَّهِ هُزُوًا ٩
They follow the messenger, the unlettered prophet. 7: 157	يَتَّبِعُونَ الرَّسُولَ النَّبِىَّ الْأُمِّىَّ ١٠
The believers do not take the unbelievers as protectors beside the believers. 3: 28	لَا يَتَّخِذِ الْمُؤْمِنُونَ الْكَافِرِينَ أَوْلِيَاءَ مِنْ دُونِ الْمُؤْمِنِينَ ١١
Did you say to people, Take me and my mother as two gods? 5: 116	أَأَنْتَ قُلْتَ لِلنَّاسِ اتَّخِذُونِى وَأُمِّى إِلَـهَيْنِ ١٢
So judge between people with the Truth and do not follow caprice. 38: 26	فَاحْكُمْ بَيْنَ النَّاسِ بِالْحَقِّ وَ لَا تَتَّبِعِ الْهَوَى ١٣
Indeed, with you We are listening. 26: 15	إِنَّا مَعَكُمْ مُسْتَمِعُونَ ١٤
On that day, (some) faces shall be radiant and (some) faces shall be dark. 3: 106	■ يَوْمَ تَبْيَضُّ وُجُوهٌ وَتَسْوَدُّ وُجُوهٌ ١٥

Notes for text above

■ *Line 8:* إِلَـهَهُ is accusative and is translated '*as his god*'. This use of the accusative is known as a *hal* construction. See also line 9 - هُزُوًا '*as a joke*' and line 12 - إِلَـهَيْنِ '*as two gods*'.

■ *Line 15:* The Form IX verb is used mainly for colours

and defects. The past tense is on the pattern of

اِحْمَرَّ, *he became red/he blushed* from the

adjective أَحْمَرُ, *red*. The present tense is on the

pattern of يَحْمَرُّ, *he blushes*.

تَسْوَدُّ and تَبْيَضُّ are two examples of this Form.

This is a commonly used Form and often denotes asking, taking or using for oneself the idea contained in the root verb.

Form X - Past
All Form X verbs in the past tense are formed by placing a sukun on the first root letter of the verb and prefixing this by اِسْتَـ . The alif at the beginning takes a hamzatu-l wasl.

Form I   he ate, tasted   طَعِمَ   غَفَرَ   he forgave

Form X   he asked for food   اِسْتَطْعَمَ   اِسْتَغْفَرَ   he asked for forgiveness

The suffixes of a Form X verb in the past are the same as for all verbs in the past.

Form X - Present
The Present active of all Form X verbs follows the same pattern:
   i. The vowel on the first prefixed letter has a fat-hah;
   ii. The vowel with the second root letter is a kasrah;
   iii. The suffixes are the same as for a Form I verb in the present.

Past Active	he sought forgiveness	اِسْتَغْفَرَ	اِسْتَعَانَ	he sought help
Present Active	he seeks forgiveness	يَسْتَغْفِرُ	يَسْتَعِينُ	he seeks help
Imperative	Seek forgiveness!	اِسْتَغْفِرْ	اِسْتَعِينُوا	Seek help! - pl.

Examples of active and passive participles and the verbal noun:

Active participle	one who seeks forgiveness	مُسْتَغْفِر	مُسْتَعِين	one who seeks help
Passive Participle	one from whom forgiveness is sought	مُسْتَغْفَر	مُسْتَعَان	one from whom help is sought
Verbal Noun	seeking forgiveness	اِسْتِغْفَار	اِسْتِعَانَة	seeking help

Meaning Patterns
A Form X verb often denotes asking, taking or using for oneself the idea contained in the root verb - as in example (i) below. It may also have the idea of 'considering' as in example (ii) below:

(i) اِسْتَغْفَرَ he asked for forgiveness - from غَفَرَ , he forgave

(ii) اِسْتَحْسَنَ he considered good, he approved - from حَسُنَ , it was good, fine

خَرَّ he fell down	اِسْتَطَاعَ / يَسْتَطِيعُ	he was able/he is able
قَرْيَة a town, village	مَائِدَة	a table, a meal
هَوَى / يَهْوِى to desire	أَجَل	a term

The fruits of Salat
We are commanded to seek God's help through reliance on sabr and immersion in Prayer. The human being is prone to mood swings between exultation and despair. Life is both a source of enjoyment and a long test. Often problems seem to be so many and so never-ending. The only real solution is to be always optimistic of God's guidance and grace. This is the source of sabr and the fruit of regular Salat.

1 ■ فَاسْتَغْفَرَ رَبَّهُ وَخَرَّ رَاكِعًا

So he asked his Sustainer for forgiveness and fell down in prostration. 38: 24

2 وَسَجَدَ الْمَلَائِكَةُ كُلُّهُمْ أَجْمَعُونَ

And the angels prostrated, all of them together. 38: 74

3 حَتَّى إِذَا أَتَيَا أَهْلَ الْقَرْيَةِ اسْتَطْعَمَا أَهْلَهَا فَأَبَوْا

...Till, when they both reached the people of a village and asked its people for food, but they fused. 18: 77

4 أَفَكُلَّمَا جَاءَكُمْ رَسُولٌ بِمَا لَا تَهْوَى أَنْفُسُكُمُ اسْتَكْبَرْتُمْ

Is it not so, that everytime a messenger came to you with what you yourselves do not like, you became arrogant? 2: 87

5 ■ وَلَقَدْ جَاءَهُمْ مُوسَى بِالْبَيِّنَاتِ فَاسْتَكْبَرُوا فِى الْأَرْضِ

And Musa came to them with clear teachings (but) they remained arrogant on earth. 29: 39

6 هَلْ يَسْتَطِيعُ رَبُّكَ أَنْ يُنَزِّلَ عَلَيْنَا مَائِدَةً مِنَ السَّمَاءِ

Could your Sustainer send down on us a repast from heaven? 5: 113

7 سَوْفَ اسْتَغْفِرُ لَكُمْ رَبِّى إِنَّهُ هُوَ الْغَفُورُ الرَّحِيمُ

I shall ask my Sustainer forgiveness for you - indeed He is the Forgiving, Merciful. 12: 98

8 ■ إِيَّاكَ نَسْتَعِينُ

You Alone we ask for help. 1: 5

9 فَإِذَا جَاءَ أَجَلُهُمْ لَا يَسْتَأْخِرُونَ سَاعَةً وَ لَا يَسْتَقْدِمُونَ

And when their term has come, they cannot delay it for a moment nor can they hasten (it).16: 61

10 ■ إِنْ تَسْتَغْفِرْ لَهُمْ سَبْعِينَ مَرَّةً فَلَنْ يَغْفِرَ اللَّهُ لَهُمْ

If you seek forgiveness for them seventy times, God will not forgive them. 9: 80

11 فَسَبِّحْ بِحَمْدِ رَبِّكَ وَاسْتَغْفِرْهُ إِنَّهُ كَانَ تَوَّابًا

So celebrate the praise of your Sustainer, and seek His forgiveness. Indeed, He is Ever Forgiving. 110: 3

12 وَاسْتَعِينُوا بِالصَّبْرِ وَالصَّلَوةِ

Seek help in patience and Prayer. 2: 45

13 ■ وَاذْكُرُوا إِذْ أَنْتُمْ قَلِيلٌ مُسْتَضْعَفُونَ فِى الْأَرْضِ

And remember when you were few and weak on earth. 8: 26

14 إِنَّهُ لَا يُحِبُّ الْمُسْتَكْبِرِينَ

Indeed He does not like the arrogant ones. 6: 23

15 وَمَا كَانَ اسْتِغْفَارُ إِبْرَاهِيمَ لِأَبِيهِ إِلَّا عَنْ مَوْعِدَةٍ

And Ibrahim's seeking of forgiveness for his father was only due to a promise.. 9: 114

Notes for text above

■ *Line 1:* The initial alif of the Form X verb takes a hamzatu -l wasl and so is not pronounced when it is linked in pronunciation to a previous letter and vowel.

■ *Line 5:* 'Could your Sustainer...' has the sense of 'Would your Sustainer...'

■ *Line 8:* نَسْتَعِينُ is derived from عَانَ/ يَعِينُ , he helped/he helps from which the verbal noun is

. عَوْنٌ , help. The root letters are: ع و ن

■ *Line 10:* سَبْعِينَ مَرَّةً , 'seventy times' is an idiom used in Arabic to mean '*many times*'.

■ *Line 13:* مُسْتَضْعَفِينَ is the passive participle, plural, lit. ' those who are considered weak'. Notice the fat-hah on the second root letter.

■ *Line 14:* مُسْتَكْبِرِينَ is the active participle, plural and accusative. Notice the kasrah on the 2nd root letter.

Unit 37

More on accusative endings

We have already learnt that the accusative is used as a direct object of a verb. We also have had some examples of the accusative being used as adverbs of time and manner.

In this Unit, we give some more examples of the ways in which the accusative is used in Arabic.

i. Direct objects

You identify a direct object by asking 'whom' or 'what' after the verb.

وَخَلَقَ الَّيْلَ وَالنَّهَارَ وَالشَّمْسَ وَالقَمَرَ He created the night and the day, the sun and the moon.

All the nouns in the above are in the accusative because they are direct objects.

ii. Adverbs of time

A word which has some element of time is put in the accusative to express an adverb of time:

at morning and evening	بُكْرَةً وَأَصِيلاً	لَيْلاً وَنَهَارًا	by night and day
on the day of Resurrection	يَوْمَ القِيَامَةِ	اليَوْمَ	today
during the journey of winter	رِحْلَةَ الشِّتَاءِ	غَدًا	tomorrow

iii. Ḥāl

The word حَـال means condition or circumstance. The word is used in Arabic grammar for the condition or the circumstance at the time when the action of the main verb is taking place. The ḥāl is often expressed by a noun in the accusative. The words قِيَامًا *while* standing, and قُعُودًا *while* sitting, in line 7 opposite are accusative and are examples of a ḥāl construction.

Other examples of a ḥāl construction is the word حَمَّالَةَ *as* the carrier, in Surah al-Masad and أَفْوَاجًا *in* crowds, in Surah an-Nasr:

وَامْرَأَتُهُ حَمَّالَةَ الـحَطَبِ And his wife, **as** the carrier of firewood. 111: 4

يَدْخُلُونَ فِى دِينِ اللَّهِ أَفْوَاجًا They enter into the religion of God *in* crowds. 110: 2

iv. Specification

A noun in the accusative is used to specify in which way a verb or adjective is applied. It contains the idea of '*with regard to*' or '*in*'. For example, the word عِلْمًا below has the meaning of 'with regard to knowledge' or 'in knowledge':

رَبِّ زِدْنِى عِلْمًا *My Sustainer, increase me in knowledge.* See lines 10 and 11 opposite for more examples.

v. Absolute accusatives

A verbal noun in the accusative is placed after its own verb to show that an action is fully completed:

فَصَّلْنَاهُ تَفْصِيلاً We have explained it completely. 17: 2

تَفْصِيلاً is the verbal noun of فَصَّلَ which is a Form II verb; notice the pattern. تَفْصِيلاً is called مَفْعُولٌ مُطْلَقٌ or an 'absolute accusative'.

An absolute accusative may be qualified by an adjective to give added strength to the expression. An example of this is حُبًّا جَمًّا *with boundless love*, in line 15 opposite.

vi. Accusative for expressing aim or purpose

For examples of this type of accusative, see line 4 opposite.

The word حَال means

condition or circumstance. The word is used in Arabic grammar for the condition or the circumstance at the time when the action of the main verb is taking place. The ḥāl is often expressed by a noun in the accusative.

They leave you standing
While the noble Prophet, peace be on him, was in the middle of a Friday khutbah, a trade caravan arrived in town. The bulk of the congregation heard the commotion and rushed out of the mosque leaving the Prophet standing (line 8 opposite) and preaching.
The incident shows that even true believers are sometimes prone to overlook religious obligations and go for 'worldly gain' or 'a passing delight'. In what follows, the Qur'an reminds us that 'what is with God is better than all leisure and all trade'.

This day I have perfected for you your religion. 5: 3	١ الْيَوْمَ أَكْمَلْتُ لَكُمْ دِينَكُمْ
And Allah will judge between you on the Day of Resurrection. 4: 141	٢ فَاللَّهُ يَحْكُمُ بَيْنَكُم يَومَ الْقِيَامَةِ
And remember the name of your Lord at morn and evening. 76: 25	٣ وَاذْكُرِ اسْمَ رَبِّكَ بُكْرَةً وَ أَصِيلاً
Then Pharoah and his soldiers pursued them out of oppression and tyranny. 10: 90	■ ٤ فَأَتْبَعَهُمْ فِرْعَوْنُ وَجُنُودُهُ بَغْيًا وَعَدْواً
They exchanged God's favour for disbelief. 14: 28	٥ بَدَّلُوا نِعْمَةَ اللَّهِ كُفْرًا
And the servants of the Beneficent are those who walk gently on earth. 25: 63	٦ وَعِبَادُ الرَّحْمَـٰنِ الَّذِينَ يَمْشُونَ عَلَى الْأَرْضِ هَوْنًا
They remember God standing and sitting. 3: 191	٧ وَذَكَرُوا اللَّهَ قِيَامًا وَقُعُودًا
And they left you standing. 62: 11	٨ وَتَرَكُوكَ قَائِمًا
Stand up truly devout to God. 2: 238	٩ وَقُومُوا لِلَّهِ قَانِتِينَ
In their hearts is a disease and God has increased them in disease. 2: 10	١٠ فِى قُلُوبِهِم مَرَضٌ فَزَادَهُمُ اللَّهُ مَرَضًا
I have less wealth and children than you. 18: 39	■ ١١ أَنَا أَقَلُّ مِنكَ مَالًا وَوَلَدًا
We have explained it completely. 17: 12	■ ١٢ فَصَّلْنَاهُ تَفْصِيلاً
(How is it) that We pour down water abundantly. 80: 25	١٣ أَنَّا صَبَبْنَا الْمَاءَ صَبًّا
When the earth is shaken violently. 99: 1	١٤ إِذَا زُلْزِلَتِ الْأَرْضُ زِلْزَالَهَا
And you love wealth with boundless love. 89: 20	١٥ وَتُحِبُّونَ الْمَالَ حُبًّا جَمًّا

Notes for text above

■ *Line 4:* بَغْيًا is an example of an accusative expressing aim or purpose. بَغْيًا has the sense of '*out of* oppression', and عَدْواً '*out of* tyranny'. This means that Pharoah and his forces were motivated by the desire to oppress and tyrannize.

■ *Line 11:* Literally, *I am less than you* **with regard** to *wealth and children.* These are two examples of tamyiz.

■ *Line 12:* Literally, *We have explained it an explaining.* This is an example of an absolute accusative which gives emphasis to the verb and shows that an action is complete. Other examples of absolute accusatives are in lines 13, 14, and 15.

Unit 38

Relative Pronouns

Worship your Lord Who created you.

In the above sentence, the word 'Who' is a relative pronoun. It relates to the word 'Lord' which is called the '**antecedent**'. Antecedent means the word you refer back to.

In Arabic relative pronouns must agree with their antecedents in number and gender. The relative pronouns are:

Plural	Dual	Singular	
اَلَّذِينَ	اَللَّذَانِ/اَللَّذَينِ	اَلَّذِى	m.
اَللَّائِى	اَللَّتَانِ/اَللَّتَينِ	اَلَّتِى	f.

اَلَّذِى and اَلَّتِى may mean 'who, whom, that, which, the one who'.

اَلَّذِينَ may mean 'who, those who, those whom, the ones who'.

اَلَّذِى , اَلَّتِى and اَلَّذِينَ are the forms occuring most frequently in the Qur'an.

The '**relative clause**' refers to the part of the sentence coming after the relative pronoun.

In Arabic, the relative clause must be a complete sentence on its own.

The relative clause must therefore contain a stated or implied pronoun which refers back to the antecedent. We shall call this stated or implied pronoun the '**referent**'. The relative clause in the following is underlined.

1. اُعْبُدُوا رَبَّكُمُ الَّذِى خَلَقَكُمْ

   Worship your Lord / Who / <u>He created you</u>.

2. اتَّقُوا النَّارَ الَّتِى وَقُودُهَا النَّاسُ وَالْحِجَارَة

   Beware of the fire / which / <u>its fuel is people and stones.</u>

3. صِرَاطَ الَّذِينَ أَنْعَمْتَ عَلَيهِمْ

   The path / of those whom/ <u>You have favoured them.</u>

In sentence 1 above , the relative clause is 'He created you'. The referent is 'He' which is implied in the verb خَلَقَ and this refers back to the relative pronoun الَّذِى which is masculine singular.

In sentence 2, the referent is the attached pronoun هَا which is feminine because it refers back to النَّار which is feminine. The relative pronoun الَّتِى must of course be feminine.

In 3, the referent is the attached pronoun هِمْ which is masculine plural to agree with the relative pronoun الَّذِينَ . The pronoun هِمْ is needed in the Arabic to make the relative clause a complete sentence on its own. However, in English the referent 'them' will be left out in translation.

Two special nouns

Genitive	Accusative	Nominative	
أَبِى	أَبَا	أَبُو	(father)
ذِى	ذَا	ذُو	m. s. (possessor of)
ذَاتِ	ذَاتَ	ذَاتُ	f. s. (possessor of)

The word ذُو and ذَاتُ have dual and plural forms as well. See line 13.

The words أُولُو (m.p.) and أُولَاتُ (f.p.) mean 'possessors of'. These nouns and the various forms of ذُو are always part of an إِضَافَة construction.

1 هُوَ الَّذِى أَرْسَلَ رَسُولَهُ بِالْهُدَى وَدِينِ الْحَقِّ

He is the One Who has sent His messenger with the guidance and the religion of truth. 48: 28

2 عَنِ النَّبَإِ الْعَظِيمِ الَّذِى هُمْ فِيهِ مُخْتَلِفُونَ

About the awesome news on which they disagree. 78: 2 - 3

3 ادْفَعْ بِالَّتِى هِىَ أَحْسَنُ

Repel (evil) with that which is better. 41: 34

4 ▪ مَا هَـٰذِهِ التَّمَاثِيلُ الَّتِى أَنتُمْ لَهَا عَاكِفُونَ

What are these images to which you are devoted? 21: 52

5 وَقَالَ الَّذِينَ كَفَرُوا رَبَّنَا أَرِنَا الَّذِينَ أَضَلَّانَا

And those who had rejected faith will say: 'Our Lord! Show us both those (among jinn and humans) that have led us astray. 41: 29

6 إِنْ أُمَّهَاتُهُمْ إِلَّا الـلَّـئِى وَلَدْنَهُمْ

Their mothers are none but those who gave birth to them. 58: 2

7 أَبُونَا شَيْخٌ كَبِيرٌ

Our father is an old man. 28: 23

8 مَا كَانَ مُحَمَّدٌ أَبَا أَحَدٍ مِّن رِّجَالِكُمْ وَلَكِن رَّسُولُ اللَّهِ

Muhammad is not the father of any one of your men, but is God's messenger.. 33: 40

9 ▪ وَإِنَّ رَبَّكَ لَذُو مَغْفِرَةٍ لِّلنَّاسِ عَلَى ظُلْمِهِمْ

And indeed your Sustainer is full of forgiveness for people despite their evil-doing. 13: 6

10 وَلْيُنفِقْ ذُو سَعَةٍ مِّن سَعَتِهِ

And let him who has ample means spend of his amplitude. 65: 7

11 وَءَاتِ ذَا الْقُرْبَى حَقَّهُ

And give the close relative his due. 17: 26

12 وَبِالْوَالِدَيْنِ إِحْسَانًا وَذِى الْقُرْبَى وَالْيَتَامَى وَالْمَسَاكِينِ

And (you shall be) good to parents and close relatives, to orphans and the needy. 2: 83

13 وَءَاتَى الْمَالَ عَلَى حُبِّهِ ذَوِى الْقُرْبَى وَالْيَتَامَى

And he gives wealth - despite his love for it, to close relatives and the orphans... 2: 177

14 ▪ وَتَضَعُ كُلُّ ذَاتِ حَمْلٍ حَمْلَهَا

And every woman pregnant (lit: having a burden) will put down her burden. 22: 2

15 ▪ إِنَّمَا يَتَذَكَّرُ أُولُوا الْأَلْبَـٰبِ

Only those who have minds will take heed. 39: 9

Notes for text above

▪ *Line 4:* تَمَاثِيلُ is the broken plural of تِمْثَالٌ and so is grammatically feminine singular. Its relative pronoun الَّتِى is therefore feminine and the attached pronoun هَا is of course also feminine.

▪ *Line 9:* The preposition عَلَى in عَلَى ظُلْمِهِمْ and عَلَى in عَلَى حُبِّهِ line 13 has the sense of 'despite'.

▪ *Line 14:* تَضَعُ she puts down/she will put down, is from the weak verb وضع, to put down or to give birth.

▪ *Line 15:* The word أَلْبَـٰب is plural of لُبّ which means *mind* or *heart* and connotes *insight and wisdom*.

Unit 39

More on broken plurals

In Unit 6, we referred briefly to broken plurals of nouns and noted that many such plurals are formed according to patterns. Some of these plurals take tanwin. Some do not take tanwin. Here we give some examples of these patterns using the root letters فَعَلَ :

Broken plurals with tanwin:

Plural	Singular		Plural	Singular
(i) On the pattern of أَفْـعَـالٌ :			(ii) On the pattern of فُـعُـولٌ :	
أَوْلَادٌ	وَلَدٌ		نُفُوسٌ	نَفْسٌ
أَسْوَاقٌ	سُوقٌ		قُلُوبٌ	قَلْبٌ
(iii) On the pattern of فُـعُـلٌ :			(iv) On the pattern of فِـعَـالٌ :	
كُتُبٌ	كِتَابٌ		جِبَالٌ	جَبَلٌ
سُبُلٌ	سَبِيلٌ		رِجَالٌ	رَجُلٌ
(v) On the pattern of أَفْـعُـلٌ :			(vi) On the pattern of فِـعْـلَانٌ :	
أَنْفُسٌ	نَفْسٌ		وِلْدَانٌ	وَلَدٌ
أَعْيُنٌ	عَيْنٌ		صِبْيَانٌ	صَبِيٌّ

Broken plurals without tanwin:

Plural	Singular		Plural	Singular
(i) On the pattern of فُـعَـلَاءُ :			(ii) On the pattern of أَفْـعِـلَاءُ :	
عُلَمَاءُ	عَالِمٌ		أَنْبِيَاءُ	نَبِيٌّ
فُقَرَاءُ	فَقِيرٌ		أَغْنِيَاءُ	غَنِيٌّ
(iii) On the pattern of فَـعَـالِلُ :			(iv) On the pattern of فَـعَـالِيلُ :	
مَسَاجِدُ	مَسْجِدٌ		تَمَاثِيلُ	تِمْثَالٌ
مَسَاكِنُ	مَسْكَنٌ		مَحَارِيبُ	مِحْرَابٌ

In the indefinite, broken plurals without tanwin end with a single fat-hah for both the accusative and genitive. In line 13 opposite, the words *maḥariba* and *tamathila* both end with a fat-hah but they are genitive. You will remember that certain proper names also have the same ending for both the accusative and genitive, for example: *Maryama*, *Fir'awna*.

Remember that: Broken plurals of nouns referring to non-rational beings or things are considered to be gramatically **feminine singular**. This means that:

i. the adjective of such a broken plural noun will be feminine singular. In line 5 opposite, for example, the adjectives *mutahharatan* and *qayyimatun* are singular whereas the nouns they qualify are plural.

ii. the pronouns used to refer to a broken plural noun will be feminine singular: see the attached pronoun *haa* in lines 3, 5, 8, 12, and 15 opposite.

iii. if the broken plural is the subject of a verb, the verb will be feminine singular. For example, see the verbs *tatma'innu* in line 1, and *zuwwijat* in line 6.

1 أَلَا بِذِكْرِ اللَّهِ تَطْمَئِنُّ الْقُلُوبُ

Surely, in the remembrance of God hearts do find rest. 13: 28

2 قَالَتْ إِنَّ الْمُلُوكَ إِذَا دَخَلُوا قَرْيَةً أَفْسَدُوهَا

She said: Indeed kings - when they enter a town, they corrupt it. 27: 34

3 وَالْخَيْلَ وَالْبِغَالَ وَالْحَمِيرَ لِتَرْكَبُوهَا وَزِينَةً

And (He created) horses and mules and donkeys that you might ride them and as an adornment 16: 8

4 رِجَالٌ لَا تُلْهِيهِمْ تِجَارَةٌ وَلَا بَيْعٌ عَنْ ذِكْرِ اللَّهِ

Men - neither bargaining nor selling diverts them from the remembrance of God. 24: 37

5 ▪ رَسُولٌ مِنَ اللَّهِ يَتْلُو صُحُفًا مُطَهَّرَةً فِيهَا كُتُبٌ قَيِّمَةٌ

A messenger from God reciting pages purified in which are sound prescriptions. 98: 2-3

6 ▪ وَإِذَا النُّفُوسُ زُوِّجَتْ

And when (all) human beings are coupled (with their deeds)... 81: 7

7 ▪ وَمَا ظَلَمْنَاهُمْ وَلَكِنْ كَانُوا أَنْفُسَهُمْ يَظْلِمُونَ

And We did not wrong them but they have been wronging themselves. 16: 118

8 لَهُمْ قُلُوبٌ لَا يَفْقَهُونَ بِهَا وَلَهُمْ أَعْيُنٌ لَا يُبْصِرُونَ بِهَا

And they have hearts with which they do not grasp the truth and they have eyes with which they do not see. 7: 179

9 وَقَالُوا رَبَّنَا إِنَّا أَطَعْنَا سَادَتَنَا وَكُبَرَاءَنَا فَأَضَلُّونَا السَّبِيلَ

And they will say: Our Sustainer! Indeed We obeyed our leaders and our great ones and they led us astray from the right path. 33: 67

10 إِنَّمَا يَخْشَى اللَّهَ مِنْ عِبَادِهِ الْعُلَمَاءُ

Only the ones with knowledge among His servants fear God. 35: 28

11 لَقَدْ سَمِعَ اللَّهُ قَوْلَ الَّذِينَ قَالُوا إِنَّ اللَّهَ فَقِيرٌ وَنَحْنُ أَغْنِيَاءُ

God has indeed heard the saying of those who said, God is poor and we are rich. 3: 181

12 وَمَسَاجِدُ يُذْكَرُ فِيهَا اسْمُ اللَّهِ كَثِيرًا

And mosques - in them the name of God is remembered much. 22: 40

13 ▪ يَعْمَلُونَ لَهُ مَا يَشَاءُ مِنْ مَحَارِيبَ وَتَمَاثِيلَ وَجِفَانٍ

They (were) making for him whatever he wished of sanctuaries, and images, and basins...

14 كَالْجَوَابِ وَقُدُورٍ رَاسِيَاتٍ

as (large as) watering-troughs and cauldrons firmly anchored. 34: 13

15 مَا هَذِهِ التَّمَاثِيلُ الَّتِي أَنْتُمْ لَهَا عَاكِفُونَ

What are these images to which you are devoted? 21: 52

Notes for text above

▪ **Line 5**: The word صُحُف literally means 'pages' and here refers to 'revelations'. It is the plural of صَحِيفَة . The word كُتُب is normally translated as books or scriptures. Here it may be translated as prescriptions or ordinances. The singular is كِتَاب . The root word has the basic meaning of to write or to prescribe.

▪ **Line 6 & 7**: Notice that the word نَفْس has two broken plurals: نُفُوس here meaning human beings or souls and أَنْفُس meaning selves.

▪ **Line 13:** The words تَمَاثِيل and مَحَارِيب are both genitive because they are controlled by a preposition. Notice however that they both end with a fat-hah.

Unit 40

Conditional Sentences

Note carefully
The use of the Past form of the verb in Arabic should not be taken automatically to refer to an event that has happened. You must look at the context in which a verb is used to determine its tense.

Parts of a conditional sentence

إِن تَنصُرُوا اللَّهَ يَنصُرْكُمْ If you help (the cause of) God, He will help you. 47:7

The above sentence is known as a conditional sentence. It is made up of two parts. The first part is: 'If you help the cause of God'. It begins with the word 'if'. This part is known as the condition and is called the شَرْط in Arabic.

The second part of the sentence is 'He will help you'. This part is the fulfilment of the condition. In Arabic it is called the جَوَاب or reply to the condition. In Arabic conditional sentences, the شَرْط *condition*, almost always comes before the جواب *reply* .

Introducing the condition

There are various short words or particles used in Arabic for 'if' . The most common of these are: إِذَا , لَوْ and إِنْ .

لَوْ is often used for hypothetical conditions. See line 3 opposite.

إِذَا may be translated as 'when' or 'whenever'. إِذَا must be distinguished from لَمَّا .

لَمَّا does not introduce a conditional sentence but is clearly used to introduce a verb in the past tense. Compare the following two examples:

. . . إِذَا جَاءَكَ الْمُنَافِقُونَ قَالُوا نَشْهَدُ When the hypocrites come to you,
they say, 'We testify...' 63: 1

وَلَمَّا جَاءَهُمُ الْحَقُّ قَالُوا هَـٰذَا سِحْرٌ مُبِينٌ When the Truth came to them,
they said, 'This is plain magic.' 43:30

There are other particles used to introduce conditional sentences. The most common of these in the Qur'an is مَنْ :

مَنْ may have the meaning of 'whoever, he who, those who';

كُلَّمَا - whenever; أَيْنَمَا - wherever.

Submitting your face
Whoever submits his face to God and is a doer of good.. (line 10) opposite. Here 'his face' has the meaning of 'his whole self'. This is an example of metonomy - a figure of speech in which the part is used to express the whole. The face has the marvellous capacity to reflect the range of emotions and human states—happiness, fear, grief, anger, hurt, pain, calm reflection. It can, quite dangerously, also dissimulate and cover up and be a front for hypocrisy and deviousness.
In contrast, the use of the word face in 'face of God' cannot be taken to represent human emotions but is a pointer to God's existence and his vast and awesome creative power.

Verbs in conditional sentences
Arabic uses either the Past form of the verb or the Jussive for conditional sentences.
   i. the past form may be used in both the shart and the jawab - see lines 1, 2, 3, 7 and 13 opposite;
   ii. the jussive may be used in both the shart and the jawab - see lines 5, 6 and 14;
   iii. there may be a mixture of the past form and the jussive in the jawab and the shart - see line 12;
   iv. the jawab may have an imperative - see line 8;
   v. the shart may not have a verb at all - see line 4;
   vi. the jawab may not have a verb at all - see line 10.

Introducing the jawab
The jawab is often introduced by *la* or *fa* - both of which can remain untranslated.
If the condition is introduced by *lau* , the jawab is often introduced by *la* - see lines 1, 2, 3 and 5 opposite.
The jawab is introduced by *fa* if:
   i. the jawab begins with anything but a verb - see line 9;
   ii. the jawab begins with a verb in the imperative - see line 8.

1	لَوْ أَنْزَلْنَا هَـٰذَا الْقُرْءَانَ عَلَى جَبَلٍ	If We had sent down this Qur'an on a mountain..,
2	لَرَأَيْتَهُ خَاشِعًا مُتَصَدِّعًا مِنْ خَشْيَةِ اللَّهِ	...you would have seen it humbling itself, breaking asunder out of the awe of God. 59: 21
3	وَلَوْ شَاءَ رَبُّكَ لَجَعَلَ النَّاسَ أُمَّةً وَاحِدَةً	If your Lord had wished, he would have made human beings one nation. 11: 118
4	وَلَوْلَا فَضْلُ اللَّهِ عَلَيْكُمْ وَرَحْمَتُهُ لَكُنْتُمْ مِنَ الْخَاسِرِينَ	And if it were not for the grace of God on you and His mercy, you would have been among the losers. 2: 64
5	إِنْ تَنْصُرُوا اللَّهَ يَنْصُرْكُمْ	If you help (the cause of) God, He will help you. 47:7
6	إِنْ تُطِيعُوهُ تَهْتَدُوا	If you obey him (the messenger) , you will be guided. 24: 54
7	وَإِذَا خَاطَبَهُمُ الْجَاهِلُونَ قَالُوا سَلَامًا	And when the ignorant ones address them, they say, Peace. 25: 63
8	فَإِذَا قُضِيَتِ الصَّلَـٰوةُ فَانْتَشِرُوا فِى الْأَرْضِ	And when the Salat is ended, then disperse in the land. 62: 10
9	مَنْ تَبِعَ هُدَاىَ فَلَا خَوْفٌ عَلَيْهِمْ وَ لَا هُمْ يَحْزَنُونَ	Whoever follows my guidance, there shall be no fear on them and they shall not grieve. 2: 38
10■	مَنْ أَسْلَمَ وَجْهَهُ لِلَّهِ وَهُوَ مُحْسِنٌ فَلَهُ أَجْرُهُ عِنْدَ رَبِّهِ	Whoever submits his face to God and is a doer of good, he shall have his reward with his Lord. 2: 112
11■	وَمَنْ يَشْكُرُ فَإِنَّمَا يَشْكُرُ لِنَفْسِهِ	And whoever is grateful, he is only grateful for the benefit of his own self. 31: 12
12	فَمَنْ شَهِدَ مِنْكُمُ الشَّهْرَ فَلْيَصُمْهُ	Whoever from among you witnesses the month (of Ramadan), let him fast it. 2: 185
13	كُلَّمَا دَعَوْتُهُمْ لِتَغْفِرَ لَهُمْ جَعَلُوا أَصَابِعَهُمْ فِى ءَاذَانِهِمْ	Whenever I invited them for you to forgive them, they put their fingers in their ears. 71 : 7
14	أَيْنَ مَا تَكُونُوا يَأْتِ بِكُمُ اللَّهُ جَمِيعًا	Wherever you may be, Allah will bring you forth, all (of you). 2: 148
15■	فَأَيْنَمَا تُوَلُّوا فَثَمَّ وَجْهُ اللَّهِ	So wherever you turn, there is the face of God. 2: 115

Notes for text above

■ **Line 10:** وَجْهَهُ 'his face' has the meaning of 'his whole self'. This is an example of a figure of speech in which the part is used to express the whole.

■ **Line 11:** The preposition لِ in لِنَفْسِهِ has the meaning of 'for the benefit of'.

■ **Line 15:** This verse should not be taken to mean that God is part of His creation or that the creation is part of God. Instead the creation provides marvellous evidence of the creative power of God and His existence.

Word List 2

بَعَثَ / يَبْعَثُ — to send; to raise up

الْبَعْثُ — the Resurrection

ابْتَغَى / يَبْتَغِي — VIII. to desire, seek

بَلَغَ / يَبْلُغُ — to reach, attain

بَلَاغٌ — a communication, warning

بَيْتٌ / بُيُوتٌ — house; family /pl.

ا

إِثْمٌ — sin, guilt

أَثِيمٌ — a wicked person

أَجَلٌ — a fixed term; a cause

أَحَدٌ — one

إِحْدَى — one (f.)

أَخٌ / إِخْوَانٌ - إِخْوَةٌ — brother/pl.

أُخْتٌ — sister

أَذِنَ / يَأْذَنُ — to permit

إِذْنٌ — permission

أَلِيمٌ — painful

أُمَّةٌ / أُمَمٌ — a people, community, nation/pl.

أَمِنَ / يَأْمَنُ — to be secure

أَمِينٌ — trustworthy, secure

أَوَّلُ / أَوَّلُونَ — first/pl.

أُولَى — first (f.)

أَيٌّ — who, what, which?

ت

تَحْتَ — under, beneath

تَلَى / يَتْلُو — to follow; to read, declare

تَابَ / يَتُوبُ (إِلَى) — to repent (to God)

تَابَ (عَلَى) — to relent (to people)

التَّوَّابُ — The Relenting (Forgiving) (attribute of God)

تَوْبَةٌ — repentance

ج

أَجْرَمَ / يُجْرِمُ — IV. to be guilty of sin

مُجْرِمٌ / مُجْرِمُونَ — (act. part. of IV.) sinner, criminal/pl.

جَرَى / يَجْرِي — to run, flow; to happen

تَجْرِي — it flows; they flow

جَهَنَّمُ — hell (f.)

ب

بَأْسٌ — force, severity, evil

بَأْسَاءُ — trouble, misfortune

بِئْسَ — bad, miserable

بَشَّرَ / يُبَشِّرُ — II. to give good news, to announce

بُشْرَى — good news

بَشِيرٌ — a bringer of good news

ح

أَحَبَّ / يُحِبُّ — to love, like

حُبٌّ — love

حَبٌّ	grain; corn (coll.)
حَبَّةٌ	a grain
حَرَّمَ / يُحَرِّمُ	II. to forbid; make unlawful
حَرَامٌ	prohibited; sacred
حَلَّ / يَحِلُّ	to be lawful
أَحَلَّ / يُحِلُّ	IV. to make lawful
حَلَالٌ	lawful
الْحَمْدُ	All (lit. the) praise
الْحَمِيدُ	the Praised One (attribute of God)
حَمَلَ / يَحْمِلُ	to carry
حَمَّلَ / يُحَمِّلُ	II. to impose a burden
حِمْلٌ / أَحْمَالٌ	a burden; foetus/pl.
حِينٌ	a time
حِينَ	when, at the time of

خ

خَبَرٌ / أَخْبَارٌ	news, report/pl.
الْخَبِيرُ	the Aware, Knowing (attribute of God)
خَسِرَ / يَخْسَرُ	to suffer loss; to perish
خُسْرٌ	loss
خَاسِرُونَ	losers
يَخْلُدُ	to live forever
خَالِدٌ / خَالِدُونَ	living forever/pl.
أَخْلَدَ	IV. to make live forever
الْخُلْدُ	eternity

د

دِينٌ	religion; judgment
الدِّينُ	the true faith, religion; judgment
دَيْنٌ	a debt

ذ

ذَاقَ / يَذُوقُ	to taste; to experience
أَذَاقَ / يُذِيقُ	IV. to cause to taste

ر

رَجُلٌ / رِجَالٌ	a man/men
رَدَّ / يَرُدُّ	to drive back; to avert
اِرْتَدَّ / يَرْتَدُّ	VIII. to return; to turn back
رَضِيَ / يَرْضَى	to be content, pleased
رِضْوَانٌ	pleasure, grace

ز

زَكَّى / يُزَكِّى	II. to purify
تَزَكَّى / يَتَزَكَّى	V. to try to be pure; to give in charity
الزَّكٰوةُ	Zakat, the purifying tax
زَوَّجَ / يُزَوِّجُ	II. to give in marriage; to join together
زَوْجٌ / أَزْوَاجٌ	spouse (husband or wife); one of a pair; a species /pl.
زَوْجَانِ / زَوْجَيْنِ	two pairs; two kinds, two individuals paired together

زَادَ / يَزِيدُ	to increase
اِزْدَادَ / يَزْدَادُ	VIII. to increase, suffer an increase
زِيَادَةٌ	an increase
مَزِيدٌ	increase, addition

شَاكِرٌ	one who gives thanks, grateful person
الشَّاكِرُ	(attribute of God) Grateful and giving rewards to people for their obedience
مَشْكُورٌ	gratefully accepted, acceptable

س

سَبَّحَ / يُسَبِّحُ	II. to celebrate the praise of; to glorify
تَسْبِيحٌ	act of praising, glorification
سُبْحَانَ اللّٰهِ	Glory be to God!
سَجَدَ / يَسْجُدُ	to prostrate
سَاجِدٌ / سَاجِدُونَ	(act. part.) prostrating; one who prostrates/pl.
سُجُودٌ	prostration
مَسْجِدٌ / مَسَاجِدُ	a place or time of prostration, masjid/pl.
سَحَرَ / يَسْحَرُ	to enchant, bewitch
سِحْرٌ	sorcery, magic
سَاحِرٌ / سَحَرَةٌ	sorcerer/pl.
سَمَّى / يُسَمِّى	II. to name
مُسَمًّى	named, fixed
اِسْمٌ / أَسْمَاءُ	name/names

ش

شَجَرٌ	trees (coll. noun)
شَكَرَ / يَشْكُرُ	to give thanks, to be grateful
شُكْرٌ ـ شُكُورٌ	gratitude, giving thanks

ص

صَلَّى / يُصَلِّى	II. to pray, perform Salat
صَلَّى عَلَى	to bless
اَلصَّلٰوةُ	the Salat; the Prayer
صَلَوَاتٌ	blessings, mercies; (22: 41) synagogues
مُصَلٍّ / مُصَلُّونَ	one who prays
مُصَلًّى	a place of prayer
أَصَابَ / يُصِيبُ	IV. to befall, to happen; to strike, injure

ض

ضَرَبَ / يَضْرِبُ	to hit, strike, (but used with a variety of meanings)
ضَرَّ / يَضُرُّ	to injure
ضَيْرٌ	injury, harm

ط

طَيِّبٌ / طَيِّبُونَ	good, wholesome; a good person (m.) /pl.
طَيِّبَةٌ / طَيِّبَاتٌ	good, wholesome; a good person (f.) /pl.

ظ

ظَنَّ / يَظُنُّ	to think, imagine
ظَنٌّ	opinion, suspicion
ظَهَرَ / يَظْهَرُ	to appear
ظَهَرَ عَلَى	to ascend; to distinguish
ظَاهَرَ / يُظَاهِرُ	III. to assist
أَظْهَرَ / يُظْهِرُ	IV. to cause to appear
أَظْهَرَ عَلَى	to make (someone) acquainted with
ظَهْرٌ / ظُهُورٌ	a back
ظَاهِرٌ	manifest, clear, outward (opposite of batin)

ع

عَدَّ / يَعُدُّ	to count
أَعَدَّ	IV. to prepare, arrange
عَدَدٌ	a number
عِدَّةٌ	a number; prescribed term
عَرَضَ	to display, set before
عَرَضٌ	breadth, extent; temporal goods
أَعْرَضَ / يُعْرِضُ	IV. to turn aside, refuse
إِعْرَاضٌ	a turning away, aversion, rejection
مُعْرِضُونَ	(act. part. of IV.) those who turn away
عَرَفَ / يَعْرِفُ	to know
مَعْرُوفٌ	(pass. part.) known, recognized; good, kindness
عِقَابٌ	punishment

عَاقِبَةٌ	end, result
عَلَا / يَعْلُو	to be high; to be proud
تَعَالَى	VI. May He be exalted!
الْعَلِيُّ	The Sublime, High (attribute of God)
الْأَعْلَى	The Most High
عَلَى	(prep.) on, above; against; on account of; despite
عَيْنٌ / أَعْيُنٌ	an eye / eyes
عَيْنٌ / عُيُونٌ	a spring, fountain/pl.
مَعِينٌ	clear-flowing

غ

أَغْنَى / يُغْنِي	IV. to enrich, profit; to satisfy
غَنِيٌّ / أَغْنِيَاءُ	rich, self-sufficient/pl.
الْغَنِيُّ	The Self-Sufficient (attribute of God)
الْغَيْبُ	The Unseen, the Unobservable

ف

فَتَنَ / يَفْتِنُ	to test
فِتْنَةٌ	temptation; test; discord; persecution, punishment
فَحْشَاءُ	shameful (deeds), immoral, filthy
فِرْعَوْنُ	Pharaoh
فَرَقَ / يَفْرُقُ	to split, divide; to decree
فَرَّقَ / يُفَرِّقُ	II. to split, divide, make a schism
فَرِيقٌ	a party, group

الْفُرْقَانُ	The Criterion (distinguishing between right and wrong): name of the Qur'an
تَفَرَّقَ / يَتَفَرَّقُ	V. to split from one another
افْتَرَى / يَفْتَرِى	VIII. to forge, invent
فَسَدَ / يَفْسُدُ	to be corrupt
فَسَادٌ	corruption
أَفْسَدَ / يُفْسِدُ	IV. to cause corruption
مُفْسِدٌ / مُفْسِدُونَ	(act. part. of IV.) one who acts corruptly, causes corruption/pl.
فَسَقَ / يَفْسُقُ	to disobey, to act wickedly
فِسْقٌ	transgression, wickedness
فَاسِقٌ / فَاسِقُونَ	(act. part.) transgressor, a wicked person/pl.
فُسُوقٌ	wickedness, transgression

ق

قَدَّمَ / يُقَدِّمُ	II. to send ahead (e.g. good works before Judgment Day)
تَقَدَّمَ / يَتَقَدَّمُ	V. to advance, go before
اسْتَقْدَمَ / يَسْتَقْدِمُ	X. to wish to advance
قَدَمٌ / أَقْدَامٌ	foot; merit/pl.
قَرَأَ / يَقْرَأُ	to read
الْقُرْءَانُ	the Qur'an
قَرِبَ / يَقْرَبُ	to approach, draw near to
قَرَّبَ / يُقَرِّبُ	II. to cause to draw near
اقْتَرَبَ / يَقْتَرِبُ	VIII to draw near, approach
قُرْبَى	close relationship
ذُو الْقُرْبَى	a relative

قَرِيبٌ	near
أَقْرَبُ	nearer
مُقَرَّبُونَ	those who are honoured (i.e. those permitted to draw near)
قَضَى / يَقْضِى	to decree; to complete
قُوَّةٌ	power, strength
قَوِىٌّ	strong, powerful

ك

كَسَبَ / يَكْسِبُ	to gain, acquire
اكْتَسَبَ / يَكْتَسِبُ	VIII. to seek to gain
كَلَّمَ / يُكَلِّمُ	II. to speak (to or with)
تَكَلَّمَ / يَتَكَلَّمُ	V. to speak
كَلَامٌ	a word, speech
كَلِمَةٌ / كَلِمَاتٌ	a word, a decree/pl.
كَيْفَ	how?

ل

لَيْسَ	he is not, it is not
اللَّيْلُ	the night
لَيْلاً	at night
لَيْلَةٌ / لَيَالِى	a night/pl.

م

مَتَّعَ / يُمَتِّعُ	II. to permit (s.o.) to enjoy
تَمَتَّعَ / يَتَمَتَّعُ	V. to enjoy, delight oneself

اِسْتَمْتَعَ / يَسْتَمْتِعُ	X. to enjoy; derive pleasure or advantage from
مَتَاعٌ	goods, provisions
مَسَّ / يَمُسُّ	to touch, befall
مَلَكٌ	an angel
الْمَلَائِكَةُ	the angels
مَالٌ / أَمْوَالٌ	wealth, possession/pl.

ن

نَجَّا / يُنَجِّي	II. to deliver, set free
نَجْوَى	a private conference
نَادَى / يُنَادِي	III. to call out, make a proclamation
نِدَاءٌ	a cry, proclamation
نِسَاءٌ	women
أَنْعَمَ / يُنْعِمُ	IV. to favour
نِعْمَةٌ / نِعَمٌ ـ أَنْعُمٌ	grace, favour/pl.
أَنْعَامٌ	cattle
نَفَعَ / يَنْفَعُ	to be useful, to benefit
نَفْعٌ	use, benefit, profit
مَنَافِعُ	benefits, advantages
نَافَقَ / يُنَافِقُ	III. to enter into a hole; to be a hypocrite
مُنَافِقٌ / مُنَافِقُونَ	(act. part. III.) hypocrite/pl.
نِفَاقٌ	hypocrisy
أَنْفَقَ / يُنْفِقُ	IV. to spend
إِنْفَاقٌ	spending
نَهْرٌ / أَنْهَارٌ	river/rivers
نَهَارٌ	day (as opposed to night)

نَهَى / يَنْهَى	to forbid, prohibit
اِنْتَهَى / يَنْتَهِي	VIII. to desist from, to refrain, to end

هـ

هَلَكَ / يَهْلِكُ	to perish, die
أَهْلَكَ / يُهْلِكُ	IV. to destroy, waste, cause to perish

و

وَجَّهَ / يُوَجِّهُ	II. to turn, direct
وَجْهٌ / وُجُوهٌ	face, faces
لِوَجْهِ اللَّهِ	for the sake of God
وَاحِدٌ	one
وَاحِدَةٌ	one (f.)
أَوْحَى / يُوحِي	IV. to reveal
وَحْيٌ	revelation
وَفَّى / يُوَفِّي	II. to repay in full
أَوْفَى / يُوفِي	IV. to fulfil a covenant
تَوَفَّى / يَتَوَفَّى	V. to take the life of someone; (in the passive) to die
تَوَكَّلَ / يَتَوَكَّلُ	V. to depend
وَكِيلٌ	guardian; disposer of affairs
تَوَلَّى / يَتَوَلَّى	V. to turn away
وَلِيٌّ / أَوْلِيَاءُ	friend, helper, protector/pl.

ي

يَمِينٌ	right; right hand; an oath
أَيْمَانٌ	oaths
مَيْمَنَةٌ	right hand

Word List 3

أ

أَبَداً	forever, always, ever; (with negative) never
أُمٌّ / أُمَّهَاتٌ	mother/mothers
أُمَّةٌ / أُمَمٌ	a people, community, nation/pl.
أُنْثَى / إِنَاثٌ	a female/females
أَنَّى	how, from where
آلٌ	family
أُولُوا	possessors of
أُولِى	possessors of (acc. & gen.)
أُوْلَـٰئِكَ (أولاء + ك)	those
هَـٰؤُلَاءِ (هـ + أولاء)	these
مَأْوَى	abode, refuge

ب

بَحْرٌ / بِحَارٌ ـ أَبْحُرٌ	sea/seas
بَدَّلَ / يُبَدِّلُ	II. to change, substitute
بَدَا / يَبْدُو	to appear
بِرٌّ	piety, righteousness
بَرٌّ / أَبْرَارٌ	righteous person/pl.
بَرٌّ	Most Kind (an attribute of God)
بَارَكَ / يُبَارِكُ	III. to bless
تَبَارَكَ اللَّهُ	VI. Blessed be God
بَسَطَ / يَبْسُطُ	to extend, spread; to grant
بَشَرٌ	a human being, human beings
بَطَلَ / يَبْطُلُ	to be in vain; to perish

بَاطِلٌ	false, falsehood
بَطْنٌ / بُطُونٌ	belly/pl.
بَاطِنٌ	minor part; hidden
بَلَا / يَبْلُو	to test, try
بَلَاءٌ	a trial, calamity
بَابٌ / أَبْوَابٌ	door, gate

ت

| تَرَكَ / يَتْرُكُ | to leave |
| تِلْكَ | that, those (f.) |

ث

ثَلَاثَةٌ	three
ثَمَرَةٌ / ثَمَرَاتٌ	fruit /pl.
اِثْنَانِ / اِثْنَيْنِ	two /acc. & gen.

ج

جَبَلٌ / جِبَالٌ	mountain /mountains
جَحِيمٌ	hell, hellfire
جَادَلَ / يُجَادِلُ	III. dispute, argue
جِدَالٌ	dispute, argument
جُنَاحٌ	crime; blame
جُنْدٌ / جُنُودٌ	an army, a force
جَانٌّ	a serpent; demon
الْجِنُّ	jinns
جَاهَدَ / يُجَاهِدُ	III. to strive, struggle

جِهَادٌ	striving, struggle
مُجَاهِدٌ / مُجَاهِدُونَ	(act. part. of III.) one who strives, struggles/pl.
جَهِلَ / يَجْهَلُ	to be ignorant
جَاهِلٌ / جَاهِلُونَ	(act. part.) an ignorant person/pl.
اَلْجَاهِلِيَّةُ	Ignorance: (period of) Ignorance - pre-Qur'anic period
أَجَابَ / يُجِيبُ	IV. to answer
اِسْتَجَابَ / يَسْتَجِيبُ	X. to respond
جَوَابٌ	an answer

ح

حَدِيثٌ / أَحَادِيثُ	saying; story/pl.
حَزِنَ / يَحْزُنُ	to grieve
حَزِنَ / يَحْزَنُ	to be sad
حُزْنٌ – حَزَنٌ	sorrow; grief
حَشَرَ / يَحْشُرُ	to gather; to banish
حَشْرٌ	gathering
اَلْـحَشْرُ	(the day of) Assembly (after death)
حَفِظَ / يَحْفَظُ	to keep, guard, protect
حَافِظٌ / حَافِظُونَ	(act. part.) keeper, protector/pl.
اَلْـحَفِيظُ	the Protector (attribute of God)
حَيْثُ	where, wherever
مِنْ حَيْثُ	from whence; in a manner which
أَحَاطَ / يُحِيطُ	IV. to surround; to comprehend
اَلْمُحِيطُ	The One who encompasses, comprehends (everything)

خ

أَخْزَى / يُخْزِى	IV. to disgrace
خِزْىٌ	shame, disgrace
خَشِيَ / يَخْشَى	to fear
خَشْيَةٌ	fear
خَلَصَ	to be pure, sincere
أَخْلَصَ	IV. to purify
مُخْلِصٌ / مُخْلِصُونَ	(act. part. of IV.) sincere person with pure faith/pl.

د

دَبَّرَ / يُدَبِّرُ	II. to dispose, manage
تَدَبَّرَ / يَتَدَبَّرُ	V. to meditate, reflect, consider
دُبُرٌ / أَدْبَارٌ	the back, hind part, extremity
دَرَى / يَدْرِى	to know
أَدْرِى	I know
أَدْرَى / يُدْرِى	IV. to cause to know, to teach
دَارٌ / دِيَارٌ	house, dwelling, abode /pl.

ذ

ذُرِّيَّةٌ	children, progeny
ذَنْبٌ / ذُنُوبٌ	sin; crime/pl.
ذَهَبَ / يَذْهَبُ	to go
أَذْهَبَ / يُذْهِبُ	IV. to take away
ذَهَابٌ	taking away
اَلذَّهَبُ	gold

ر

رَجَا / يَرْجُو	to hope; (with negative) to fear
رَفَعَ / يَرْفَعُ	to raise up; to exalt
رُوحٌ	spirit, soul, life
رُوحُ الْقُدُسِ	the spirit of holiness (referring to Angel Jibrīl)
رِيحٌ / رِيَاحٌ	wind; power; prosperity/pl.

ز

زَيَّنَ	II. to adorn, beautify
زِينَةٌ	adornment

س

سَخَّرَ / يُسَخِّرُ	II. to subject; to put at someone's disposal
أَسَرَّ / يُسِرُّ	IV. to conceal
سِرٌّ / أَسْرَارٌ	secret/ secrets
سِرًّا	secretly; in private
سَعَى / يَسْعَى	to run; to strive for
سَعْى	striving, hastening
سَقَى / يَسْقِى	to give drink to
سَكَنَ / يَسْكُنُ	to rest; dwell
مَسْكَنٌ / مَسَاكِنُ	a dwelling, habitation/pl.
سَكِينَةٌ	tranquility
سَلَّطَ / يُسَلِّطُ	II. to give power, authority; to make victorious
سُلْطَانٌ	power, authority; proof
اِسْتَوَى / يَسْتَوِى	VIII. to be equal; to sit firmly
سَوَاءٌ	equal; same
سَوَاءَ السَّبِيلِ	the right way
سَارَ / يَسِيرُ	to go, travel

ش

شَجَرٌ	trees (coll. noun)
شَجَرَةٌ	a tree, plant
شَرِبَ / يَشْرَبُ	to drink
شَرَابٌ	a drink
شَرٌّ	evil, bad, wicked (thing)
شَرَى / يَشْرِى	to sell, barter
اشْتَرَى / يَشْتَرِى	VIII. to buy, barter
شَيْطَانٌ / شَيَاطِينُ	satan/satans
شَعَرَ / يَشْعُرُ	to feel, perceive; to realize
يَشْعُرُونَ	they realise
تَشْعُرُونَ	you (pl.) realize
شَفَعَ / يَشْفَعُ	to intercede
شَفِيعٌ / شُفَعَاءُ	intercessor/ intercessors
شَفَاعَةٌ	intercession
الشَّمْسُ	the sun

ص

أَصْبَحَ / يُصْبِحُ	IV. to become
صُبْحٌ	morning
صَدَّ / يَصُدُّ	to turn away, prevent

صَدْرٌ / صُدُورٌ	bosom, chest, breast/pl.
صِرَاطٌ	path, way
صَرَفَ / يَصْرِفُ	to turn
صَرَّفَ / يُصَرِّفُ	II. to explain; to divert
تَصْرِيفٌ	change (of winds)
أَصَابَ / يُصِيبُ	IV. to befall, to happen; to strike, injure
مُصِيبَةٌ	calamity, misfortune
صَارَ / يَصِيرُ	to go, tend towards, incline
مَصِيرٌ	destiny, goal

ض

ضَعُفَ	to be weak
ضَعْفٌ	weakness
ضَعِيفٌ / ضُعَفَاءُ	weak, a weak person/pl.
اسْتَضْعَفَ / يَسْتَضْعِفُ	X. to take advantage of weakness, to ill-treat, exploit
مُسْتَضْعَفُونَ	the weak, exploited ones
ضَاعَفَ / يُضَاعِفُ	III. to double
أَضْعَافٌ	equal portions; doubling

ط

أَطْعَمَ / يُطْعِمُ	IV. to feed
إِطْعَامٌ	feeding
طَعَامٌ	food
طَعْمٌ	taste
طَغَى / يَطْغَى	to transgress

طُغْيَانٌ	transgression
طَاغُوتٌ	whatever is worshipped besides God; evil forces, idols
أَطْفَى / يُطْفِى	to extinguish
طَمِعَ / يَطْمَعُ	to desire
طَهَّرَ / يُطَهِّرُ	II. to purify
طَافَ / يَطُوفُ	to go around
طَائِفَةٌ	a group, a company
طَارَ / يَطِيرُ	to fly
طَائِرٌ	a flying creature; an omen

ظ

ظَلَّ	to continue
ظِلٌّ / ظُلَلٌ	shade/shades
ظِلَالٌ	shade, shadow
ظَلَمَ / يَظْلِمُ	to be unjust, to wrong, to be tyrannical
ظُلْمٌ	injustice, tyranny
ظَالِمٌ / ظَالِمُونَ	an unjust person, tyrant, wrongdoer/pl.
أَظْلَمَ / يُظْلِمُ	IV. to injure; to become dark
ظُلُمَاتٌ	darkness (lit. darknesses)

ع

عَجِبَ / يَعْجَبُ	to wonder
أَعْجَبَ / يُعْجِبُ	IV. to delight, please
عَجَبٌ	wonder
عَجِيبٌ	wonderful, strange

أَعْجَزَ / يُعْجِزُ	IV. to weaken; to frustrate
مُعْجِزٌ	(act. part. of IV) one who weakens or frustrates
عَجِلَ / يَعْجَلُ	to hasten
اسْتَعْجَلَ / يَسْتَعْجِلُ	X. to seek to hasten
الْعَاجِلَةِ	the transitory world (this world)
عَدَلَ / يَعْدِلُ	to be just
الْعَرْشُ	the Throne
عَسَى أَنْ	it may be that
عَصَى / يَعْصِى	to disobey
مَعْصِيَةٌ	disobedience
عَفَا / يَعْفُو	to forgive, pardon
عَفْوٌ	a pardon
عَفُوٌّ	Most Forgiving (attribute of God)
عَقَلَ / يَعْقِلُ	to understand, to use reason
يَعْقِلُونَ	they use reason
تَعْقِلُونَ	you (pl.) use reason
عَمِىَ / يَعْمَى	to be blind
عَمًى	blindness
عَمٍى	blind
أَعْمَى	most blind
عَهِدَ	to stipulate
عَاهَدَ	III. to make an agreement
عَهْدٌ	agreement, covenant
عَادَ / يَعُودُ	to return
أَعَادَ / يُعِيدُ	to cause to return, restore

غ

غَرَّ / يَغُرُّ	to deceive
غَرُورٌ	a deceiver
غُرُورٌ	deception; vain hope
غَضِبَ / يَغْضَبُ	to be angry
غَضَبٌ	anger
مَغْضُوبٌ	(pass. part.) angered
غَفَرَ / يَغْفِرُ	to forgive
غَفَلَ	to be heedless, negligent
غَافِلٌ / غَافِلُونَ	(act. part.) negligent, careless, heedless /pl.
غَفْلَةٌ	negligence, carelessness, heedlessness
غَلَبَ / يَغْلِبُ	to overcome, conquer
غَلَبٌ	victory, conquest
غَالِبٌ / غَالِبُونَ	(act. part.) victorious/pl.

ف

فَتَحَ / يَفْتَحُ	to open; explain or reveal: to grant (mercy or victory);
فَتْحٌ	opening; victory
فَحْشَاءُ	shameful (deeds), immoral, filthy
فَاحِشَةٌ / فَوَاحِشُ	a shameful deed; a crime; fornication or adultery/pl.
فَرِحَ / يَفْرَحُ	to be glad, to rejoice
فَصَلَ / يَفْصِلُ	to divide; to judge
فَصَّلَ / يُفَصِّلُ	II. to explain clearly
فَصْلٌ	separation, distinction

أَفْلَحَ / يُفْلِحُ	IV. to prosper, to be successful; to be happy
مُفْلِحُونَ	(act.part.of IV.) prosperous, successful ones
فَازَ / يَفُوزُ	to win, gain; to receive salvation
فَوْزٌ	victory; salvation
فَوْقَ	over, above

ق

قَبِلَ / يَقْبَلُ	to accept; to admit
أَقْبَلَ	IV. to approach
تَقَبَّلَ / يَتَقَيَّلُ	VI. to accept
قَبُولٌ	acceptance
اَلْقِبْلَةُ	Qiblah, direction
قَرْيَةٌ / قُرًى	city, town, village/pl.
أَقْسَطَ / يُقْسِطُ	IV. to be just
مُقْسِطٌ / مُقْسِطُونَ	(act. part. of IV.) a just person/pl.
أَقْسَطُ	more just
قِسْطٌ	justice, equity
قَسَمَ / يَقْسِمُ	to divide
قِسْمَةٌ	a partition; a share
أَقْسَمَ / يُقْسِمُ	IV. to make an oath
قَسَمٌ	an oath
قَصَّ / يَقُصُّ	to relate, mention
قِصَصٌ	stories
قِصَاصٌ	just retribution
قَضَى / يَقْضِى	to decree; to complete
قَطَعَ / يَقْطَعُ	to cut

قَطَّعَ / يُقَطِّعُ	II. to cut off; to divide
قَعَدَ / يَقْعُدُ	to sit; to remain at home
قُعُودٌ	sitting
قَاعِدٌ / قَاعِدُونَ	(act. part.) one who sits still, remain at home, inactive /pl.
قَلَّبَ / يُقَلِّبُ	II. to cause to turn, make succeed in turns
قَلْبٌ / قُلُوبٌ	heart, hearts
اِنْقَلَبَ / يَنْقَلِبُ	VII. to be turned about or away from; to be overthrown

ك

كَرَّمَ	II. to honour
أَكْرَمَ / يُكْرِمُ	IV. to honour
كَرِيمٌ	noble, generous
اَلْكَرِيمُ	The Most Generous (attribute of God)
كَرِهَ / يَكْرَهُ	to dislike
كَارِهُونَ	(act. part. pl.) those who dislike
أَكْرَهَ / يَكْرِهُ	IV. to compel
إِكْرَاهٌ	compulsion
كَفَى / يَكْفِى	to be enough
كَلَّا	by no means; on the contrary
كَادَ / يَكَادُ	to be on the point of; (with negative) hardly
كَادَ / يَكِيدُ	to plot
يَكِيدُ	he plots
كَيْدٌ	a plot

ل

لَبِثَ / يَلْبَثُ	to stay; to delay
لَبَسَ / يَلْبِسُ	to cover; to make obscure
لَبْسٌ	confusion
لَبِسَ / يَلْبَسُ	to wear
لِبَاسٌ	clothing, garment
لِبَاسُ الْجُوعِ	'the extremes of hunger'
لِسَانٌ / أَلْسِنَةٌ	a tongue, language, speech
لَعِبَ / يَلْعَبُ	to play, to trifle with
لَعِبٌ	a play, sport
لَعَنَ / يَلْعَنُ	to curse
لَعْنٌ	a curse
لَعْنَةٌ	a curse

م

مَدَّ / يَمُدُّ	to stretch, extend
امْرُؤٌ	a man
مَرْءٌ	a man
امْرَأَةٌ	a woman; a wife
مَرْيَمُ	Maryam
مَكَرَ / يَمْكُرُ	to plot, act deceitfully
مَكْرٌ	a plot, trick
مَلَأٌ	a company, assembly, chiefs
الْمَلَأُ الْأَعْلَى	the exalted company (i.e. the angels)
مَاءٌ	water

ن

أَنْبَتَ / يُنْبِتُ	IV. to cause to grow; to produce
نَبَاتٌ	plants, growth
نَسِيَ / يَنْسَى	to forget; to neglect
أَنْشَأَ / يُنْشِئُ	IV. to raise, produce, create
نَكَحَ / يَنْكِحُ	to marry
نِكَاحٌ	marriage
أَنْكَرَ / يُنْكِرُ	IV. to reject
مُنْكَرٌ	(pass. part. of IV.) bad, repugnant, unlawful

هـ

هَاجَرَ / يُهَاجِرُ	III. to migrate
مُهَاجِرٌ	(act. part. of III.) one who migrates
اسْتَهْزَأَ / يَسْتَهْزِئُ	X. to mock, ridicule
هُزْوٌ	a mockery, joke
هَوِيَ / يَهْوَى	to desire; to incline to
هَوًى / أَهْوَاءٌ	desire, whim, passion /pl.

و

مِيثَاقٌ (و ث ق)	a covenant, a treaty
وَدَّ / يَوَدُّ	to love, to wish
وُدٌّ	love
مَوَدَّةٌ	love, affection
الْوَدُودُ	The Loving (attribute of God)
وَذَرَ / يَذَرُ	to leave, let

ذَر	(imperative) leave!
وَرِثَ / يَرِثُ	to inherit
أَوْرَثَ / يُورِثُ	IV. to bequeath; to give as inheritance
مِيرَاثٌ	inheritance
وَرَاءَ	behind, beyond
وَزَرَ / يَزِرُ	to bear, carry
وَسِعَ / يَسَعُ	to be extensive
وَاسِعٌ	wide, extensive
اَلْوَاسِعُ	The All-embracing (attribute of God)
وَصَّى	II. to enjoin, command
وَصِيَّةٌ	a will, legacy
تَوَاصَى	VI. to enjoin one another, to encourage one another
وَضَعَ / يَضَعُ	to place, lay down, put; to give birth
وَعَظَ / يَعِظُ	to warn; to admonish
مَوْعِظَةٌ	warning, admonition
وَقَعَ / يَقَعُ	to fal; to befall
وَاقِعٌ	falling upon; that which comes to pass
وَهَبَ / يَهَبُ	to bestow, give
اَلْوَهَّابُ	The Bestower (attribute of God)
وَيْلٌ	woe, destruction
وَيْلَةٌ	shame
يَا وَيْلَتَى	Alas, my shame!

ي

يَتِيمٌ / يَتَامَى	orphan/orphans
يَسَّرَ / يُيَسِّرُ	II. to make easy, facilitate
يُسْر	ease, facility
يَسِير	easy

Pronouns

	Singular		Plural	
	Attached/Separate	With words	Attached/Separate	With words
3.m.	هو ـه / ـه he, it / him, his; it, its	عليهِ منه عليهِ	هم / هم ـهم they / them, their	عليهم منهم عليهم
3.f.	هي ـها / ـها she; it; they / her; it, its; them, their	عليها منها عليها	هن / هنّ ـهن they / them, their	عليهن منهن عليهن
2.m.	أنتَ / ـكَ you / you, your	عليك منك عليك	أنتم / ـكم you / you, your	عليكم منكم عليكم
2.f.	أنتِ / ـكِ you / you, your	عليك منك عليك	أنتن / ـكن you / you, your	عليكن منكن عليكن
1.m&f	أنا / ـي ـني I / me, my	عليّ منّي عليّ	نحن / ـنا we / us, our	علينا منّا علينا

DUAL

	Attached/Separate	With words
3.m&f	هما / ـهما they both / them, their	عليهما منهما عليهما
2.m&f	أنتما / ـكما you both / you, your	عليكما منكما عليكما

The Verb in the Past (الـمَاضِي)

	Singular	Dual	Plural
3.m.	كَتَبَ (هو) He wrote	كَتَبَا (هما) They (both) wrote	كَتَبُوا (هم) They (m) wrote
3.f.	كَتَبَتْ (هي) She wrote	كَتَبَتَا (هما) They (both) wrote	كَتَبْنَ (هنّ) They (f) wrote
2.m.	كَتَبْتَ (أنتَ) You (m) wrote	كَتَبْتُمَا (أنتما) You (both) wrote	كَتَبْتُمْ (أنتم) You (m) wrote
2.f.	كَتَبْتِ (أنتِ) You (f) wrote	كَتَبْتُمَا (أنتما) You (both) wrote	كَتَبْتُنَّ (أنتنّ) You (f) wrote
1.m&f	كَتَبْتُ (أنا) I wrote	كَتَبْنَا (نحن) We wrote	كَتَبْنَا (نحن) We wrote

The Verb in the Present (Indicative) (المُضارِع)

	Singular	Dual	Plural
3.m.	يَكْتُبُ (هو) He writes	يَكْتُبانِ (هما) They (both) write	يَكْتُبونَ (هم) They (m) write
3.f.	تَكْتُبُ (هي) She writes	تَكْتُبانِ (هما) They (both) write	يَكْتُبْنَ (هنّ) They (f) write
2.m.	تَكْتُبُ (أنت) You (m) write	تَكْتُبانِ (أنتما) You (both) write	تَكْتُبونَ (أنتم) You (m) write
2.f.	تَكْتُبينَ (أنتِ) You (f) write	تَكْتُبانِ (أنتما) You (both) write	تَكْتُبْنَ (أنتنّ) You (f) write
1.m&f	أَكْتُبُ (أنا) I write	نَكْتُبُ (نحن) We write	نَكْتُبُ (نحن) We write

Derived Forms of the Verb - Active

Form	Pattern	Past	Present Indicative	Subjunctive	Jussive	Imperative	Active Participle	Passive Participle	Verbal Noun
I	فَعَلَ	عَلِمَ	يَعْلَمُ	يَعْلَمَ	يَعْلَمْ	اِعْلَمْ	عَالِم	مَعْلُوم	عِلْم
II	فَعَّلَ	عَلَّمَ	يُعَلِّمُ	يُعَلِّمَ	يُعَلِّمْ	عَلِّمْ	مُعَلِّم	مُعَلَّم	تَعْلِيم
III	فَاعَلَ	جَاهَدَ	يُجَاهِدُ	يُجَاهِدَ	يُجَاهِدْ	جَاهِدْ	مُجَاهِد	مُجَاهَد	جِهَاد
IV	أَفْعَلَ	أَحْرَزَ	يُحْرِزُ	يُحْرِزَ	يُحْرِزْ	أَحْرِزْ	مُحْرِز	مُحْرَز	إِحْرَاز
V	تَفَعَّلَ	تَعَلَّمَ	يَتَعَلَّمُ	يَتَعَلَّمَ	يَتَعَلَّمْ	تَعَلَّمْ	مُتَعَلِّم	مُتَعَلَّم	تَعَلُّم
VI	تَفَاعَلَ	تَعَاوَنَ	يَتَعَاوَنُ	يَتَعَاوَنَ	يَتَعَاوَنْ	تَعَاوَنْ	مُتَعَاوِن	مُتَعَاوَن	تَعَاوُن
VII	اِنْفَعَلَ	اِنْصَرَفَ	يَنْصَرِفُ	يَنْصَرِفَ	يَنْصَرِفْ	اِنْصَرِفْ	مُنْصَرِف	مُنْصَرَف	اِنْصِرَاف
VIII	اِفْتَعَلَ	اِسْتَمَعَ	يَسْتَمِعُ	يَسْتَمِعَ	يَسْتَمِعْ	اِسْتَمِعْ	مُسْتَمِع	مُسْتَمَع	اِسْتِمَاع
IX	اِفْعَلَّ	اِسْوَدَّ	يَسْوَدُّ	يَسْوَدَّ	يَسْوَدَّ	اِسْوَدَّ	مُسْوَدّ	مُسْوَدّ	اِسْوِدَاد
X	اِسْتَفْعَلَ	اِسْتَفْهَمَ	يَسْتَفْهِمُ	يَسْتَفْهِمَ	يَسْتَفْهِمْ	اِسْتَفْهِمْ	مُسْتَفْهِم	مُسْتَفْهَم	اِسْتِفْهَام

Passive: The passive of all present tense forms of Derived Verbs (II - X) has a fat-hah on the second root letter.

For the further study of Qur'anic Arabic and of other written Arabic you will need to have a good Arabic-English dictionary and know how to use it.

The most thorough Arabic-English dictionary on the Qur'an is *A Dictionary and Glossary of the Koran* by John Penrice which was published in 1873.

The most widely available and the best Arabic-English dictionary is *The Hans Wehr Dictionary of Modern Written Arabic*, first published in 1961. Although it deals with modern Arabic, it can be used for words in the Qur'an as well.

To be able to use both these dictionaries properly, you will need to know something of the grammar and structure of Arabic. This textbook, *Access to Qur'anic Arabic*, should provide you with this basic knowledge.

In these dictionaries, words are listed in Arabic alphabetical order according to the letters of the root word.

To look up any word, first ask yourself what are the root letters of the word. Most words normally have three root letters. It should be fairly easy now to know that the root word of مَسَاجِد is سجد , for example.

However, it is sometimes difficult to find out what the root letters of a word are especially with words derived from weak verbs - i.e. words having أ, و or ي as root letters. For example, the root letters of مُؤْمِن are م, أ and ن.

More difficult is a word like تَضَعُ - *you put*, the root letters of which are و, ض and ع. Still more difficult is a word like قُو - *save,* the root letters of which are و, ق and ى. Such words can only be mastered with reading practice and frequent use of the Arabic dictionary.

An Entry from The Penrice Dictionary and Glossary of the Koran

For the vowel on the middle root letter of the present of the Form I or root word, Penrice gives the letters a, i and o for the fat-hah, kasrah and dammah respectively.

The abbreviation aor. stands for aorist which is an old term for the present tense.

2nd. declension refers to words which do not take tanwin and which has a final fat-hah in the indefinite for both the accusative and genitive

The Derived Forms of the verb are listed under the root word. Roman numerals I - X are used. Penrice gives the Arabic of each Derived Form together with the Roman numeral.

The active participle and the passive participle (where they occur in the Qur'an) are given with each Form.

عَلَمَ aor. i. and o. *To mark, sign;* and عَلِمَ aor. a. To know (with acc. and فِى, also with أَنَّ); to distinguish (with acc. and مِنْ); to be learned or knowing; For the difference between عَلِمَ and عَرَفَ see عَرَفَ. عِلْم n.a. Science, knowledge, learning, art; عِلْمٌ لِلسَّاعَةِ 43 v. 61, "A sign or means of knowing the last hour." عَلَمٌ A sign; Plur. أَعْلَامٌ Long mountains. عَالِمٌ part. act. One who knows, or is wise. عَلَامَةٌ A sign, mark. عَالَمِينَ oblique plur. of عَالَمٌ A world; The worlds spoken of in the Korân are taken to mean the three species of rational creatures, viz. men, genii, and angels. عَلِيمٌ Learned, knowing, wise; Plur. عُلَمَآءُ (2nd declension). عَلَّمٌ Very learned, wise or knowing. أَعْلَمُ (2nd declension) comp. form, More or most wise or knowing (with ب). مَعْلُومٌ part. pass. Known, predetermined.—عَلَّمَ II. To teach (with ب, or with double acc., or with acc. and مِنْ or بِ). مُعَلَّمٌ part. pass. Taught, instructed.—أَعْلَمَ IV. To make known.—تَعَلَّمَ V. To learn (with acc. or with مِنْ).

The Hans Wehr Dictionary

The Arabic is printed without vowels and the exact pronunciation of a word is indicated by transliteration. Long vowels are indicated by a bar over the a, i and u.

First read the Introduction in the Dictionary carefully, for transliteration styles, abbreviations used and the significance of Roman numerals in particular.

Words are listed according to the root word.

The single letter a, i or u after an entry tells you what vowel goes with the second root letter of the present tense. In the case of kataba it is 'u' which stands for a dammah. The present tense of كتب is therefore يَكْتُبُ. The verbal noun(s) of the root word is given in brackets.

Roman numerals I to X are used for the Derived Forms. But **the Arabic for each Form is not written out**. It is important therefore to know the set pattern for each Derived Form. For example, if you want to find the meaning of اكْتَتَبَ, you will need to know that this is the derived Form VIII of كتب. The active and passive participles and the verbal noun of each Form are listed separately and not under the Derived Form, as in Penrice.

An entry from **The Hans Wehr Dictionary of Modern Literary Arabic**

1. The first entry is the root word. The English infinitive 'to write' is used for the root word كتب which really means 'he wrote'. The English infinitive is also used for each Derived Form.

2. The 'u' shows that the present tense of يَكْتُبُ is كتب.

3. Verbal nouns of the root word are given in brackets.

4. يَكْتُبُ is used in the sense of 'to prescribe' in the Qur'an. A word may have a variety of meanings. The precise meaning of a word must be determined by the context in which it is used.

5. The Roman numerals indicate the various Derived Forms of the verb which are derived from the root. Forms III and VIII occur in the Qur'an.

6. Plurals are given with the singular.

7. This phrase occurs in the Qur'an.

(The column on the right in only part of the entry under *kataba* in the Hans Wehr Dictionary.)

كتب *kataba u* (*katb* كتب, *kitba* كتبة, *kitāba* كتابة) to write, pen, write down, put down in writing, note down, inscribe, enter, record, book, register (ه s.th.); to compose, draw up, indite, draft (ه s.th.); to bequeath, make over by will (ل ه s.th. to s.o.); to prescribe (على ه s.th. to s.o.); to foreordain, destine (ل or على ه s.th. to s.o.; of God); pass. *kutiba* to be fated, be foreordained, be destined (ل to s.o.) | كتب على نفسه ان to be firmly resolved to ..., make it one's duty to ...; كتب عنه to write from s.o.'s dictation; كتب كتابه (*kitābahū*) to draw up the marriage contract for s.o., marry s.o. (على to) **II** to make (ه s.o.) write (ه s.th.); to form or deploy in squadrons (ه troops) **III** to keep up a correspondence, exchange letters, correspond (ه with s.o.) **IV** to dictate (ه ه to s.o. s.th.), make (ه s.o.) write (ه s.th.) **VI** to write to each other, exchange letters, keep up a correspondence **VII** to subscribe **VIII** to write (ه s.th.); to copy (ه s.th.), make a copy (ه of s.th.); to enter one's name; to subscribe (ل for); to contribute, subscribe (ل ب money to); to be entered, be recorded, be registered **X** to ask (ه s.o.) to write (ه s.th.); to dictate (ه ه to s.o. s.th.), make (ه s.o.) write (ه s.th.); to have a copy made (ه by s.o.)

كتاب *kitāb* pl. كتب *kutub* piece of writing, record, paper; letter, note, message; document, deed; contract (esp. marriage contract); book; الكتاب the Koran; the Bible | اهل الكتاب *ahl al-k.* the people of the Book, the adherents of a revealed religion, the kitabis, i.e., Christians and Jews; كتاب الزواج *k. az-zawāj* marriage contract; كتاب الطلاق *k. at-talāq* bill of divorce; كتاب تعليمي (*ta'līmī*) textbook; كتاب الاعتماد credentials (*dipl.*); دار الكتب library

كتبي *kutubī* pl. -*ya* bookseller, book-dealer

Appendix 3

Suggestions for Further Study

This book has only been an introduction to the study of Qur'anic Arabic. The study of the Qur'an is a life-long process. There will always be something new in the Qur'an for the earnest seeker of truth.

1. Listen frequently to the recitation of the Qur'an. Stick to one reciter initially. The recitation of al-Minshawi is very exact. It also induces a proper mood for appreciating the meaning of the Qur'an.

His recitation is available on cassettes and CD.

As you listen, see how much you can understand.

Try listening to the recitation in Arabic and following a translation of the Qur'an in English. A fairly literal translation is best for this - the one by Arberry is generally quite good. (A translation like that of Muhammad Asad's which is very meticulous and stimulating may not be ideal for this.)

2. Read the Qur'an frequently. Try to have a programme for completing the recitation of the Qur'an every two or three months. Ramadan is a good time to get into regular reading habits. As you read, see how much you can understand and translate. Use a copy of the Qur'an with parallel translation.

3. Memorize as much of the Qur'an as possible, even if you do not grasp the meaning of all that you memorize. Eventually with study and effort, the meanings will unfold on you. This is a constant source of enrichment.

4. Recite what you have memorized in your Salat. Recite from various parts of the Qur'an. Many of us tend to be lazy and recite the short surahs at the end of the Qur'an in our Salat. To recite from various parts of the Qur'an will make for concentration and deeper awareness.

5. Develop your knowledge of Arabic grammar and structure. In this book, we have covered only the basic elements of the grammar and structure of Qur'anic Arabic. You will need to build on this. For further studies in grammar, Dawud Cowan's *Grammar of Modern Literary Arabic* is excellent. *First Steps in Arabic Grammar* by Muhammad Haroun and M Yasien is good for late primary and early secondary school use. It deals with modern Arabic but the essential elements of grammar are the same. It uses Arabic grammatical terms side by side with established English equivalents. This is useful for those who will eventually access Arabic from Arabic sources. One drawback is the very small Arabic typeface that is used.

6. Consult various translations of the Qur'an. No single translation can ever claim to convey the full meaning of the Qur'an or to be accurate in every respect. There will often be a variety of interpretations for a given text and a translation is often limited to choosing one interpretation. For a given verse, you may need to consult a variety of translations. The widely available ones by Muhammad Asad, Muhammad Yusuf Ali and Muhammad Marmaduke Pickthall have much to commend them. *The Message of the Qur'an* by Muhammad Asad is excellent for the more dedicated scholar who will feel amply rewarded and challenged by close scrutiny of his translation and commentary. With difficult or controversial points, it is helpful to work with a study group and to have a competent teacher. Arthur J. Arberry's *The Koran Inter-*

preted is good for a close rendering of the original and manages at the same time to be elegant and poetic. In his introduction, he wrote movingly about the effect the Qur'an had on him.

Some of the newer translations sometimes suffer from bad and off-putting English.

7. For basic meanings of words, Penrice's *Dictionary and Glossary of the Qur'an* is still the most thorough although it was written more than a century ago. It uses grammatical expressions that will be only familiar to classical scholars. In some cases, he does not fail to suppress a Christian bias and deep anti-Islamic prejudices. These two points apart, the book is still very useful and reflects a certain thoroughness and exacting standards of scholarship.

8. Learn to use reference books and material on compact disks. One reference book in Arabic is indispensable for any close study of the Qur'an and its structures. It is the *Mu'jam al Mufarras li Alfaz al-Qur'an al-Karim* compiled by Muhammad Fu'ad Abd Al-Baqi. This lists all the words in the Qur'an and where and how often they occur.

The *Mu'jam al-Alfaz wa-l A'lam al-Qur'aniyyah* by Muhammad Isma'il Ibrahim is excellent for the primary meanings of Qur'anic words. This is for more advanced users.

9. Having now a good grasp of the basic grammar and structure of Arabic and being able to consult Arabic dictionaries, try referring to and reading works in Arabic. With the help of a teacher, a systematic study of the fairly recent work, *Safwat at-Tafasir* (3 vols.) by Muhammad Ali as-Sabuni will prove most stimulating and rewarding. At least, keep it as a reference.

10. Apply your knowledge to other uses of Arabic. The basic grammar that you have acquired in studying the Qur'an is also the grammar that is used in modern standard Arabic. For those who wish to go on to broaden their knowledge of Arabic into Arabic for daily use, reading books and newspapers etc. they can start with the Arabic Linguaphone course which unfortunately is very expensive. For those interested in translating from Arabic into English, *A Week in the Middle East* is a book with parallel Arabic and English texts with the translation of a very high standard. The audio tapes accompanying the book are excellent but not easily accessible. Also, Arabic is now increasingly offered at universities and institutions throughout the world and it may be useful to attend these. Intensive courses often yield the best results.

11. Finally, keep uppermost in your mind the main purpose for studying Arabic and the Qur'an. *The Way to the Qur'an* by the late Khurram Murad is a splendid book written by someone whose life and character mirrored the Qur'an to which he was intensely devoted. This book will no doubt remind us that grammar and structure are not the purpose of studying the Qur'an but a means to accurate understanding, enrichment and guidance. Our duties to the Qur'an remain: to believe in it, to recite it, to understand it, to ponder on it, to live by it, to teach it.

Recommended books, audiocassettes, computer programmes

For finding Qur'anic references

Al-Mu'jam al-Mufahras li alfaz al-Qur'an al-Karim, by Muhammad Fu'ad Abd al-Baqi, Dar ash-Sha'b, Cairo.

Easyview Kuran Kerim (computer programme - Mac format only) by M Akif Eyler, Ankara, 1993; rapid search and find facility according to surah and verse numbers. Easy downloading. Free - Public domain software. email: eyler@trbilun.bitnet

Dictionaries

Mu'jam al-Alfaz wa-l A'lam al-Qur'aniyyah by Muhammad Isma'il Ibrahim, Dar al-Fikr al-'Arabi, Cairo, 1968

A Dictionary and Glossary of the Koran by John Penrice, first published 1873

Arabic English Dictionary - the Hans Wehr Dictionary of Modern Written Arabic (paperback), edited by J M Cowan, New York, 1976

Arabic Grammar in English

First Steps in Arabic Grammar by Yasien Mohamed & Muhammed Haron, Shuter & Shooter, Pietermaritzburg, South Africa, 1989

Modern Literary Arabic by David Cowan, Cambridge University Press, 1958

Grammar of the Arabic Language (2 vols.) by Wright, Cambridge University Press

Linguaphone Arabic Course, London, 1991

English Grammar

Basic English Grammar by Don Shiach, John Murray, London, 1995

Punctuation and Grammar by Catherine Hilton & Margaret Hyder, Letts, London, 1993

Arabic grammar and Tafsir in Arabic

Al-Farid fi 'Irab al-Qur'an al-Majid, 4 vols. by Husayn ibn Abi al-'Izz al-Hamadani (d. 643 AH), edited by Muhammad Hasan an-Nimr, Dar ath-Thaqafah, Doha, Qatar, 1991

Mu'jam Qawa'id al-Lughah al-Arabiyyah fi Jadawil wa Lawhat (A Dictionary of Arabic Grammar in Charts and Tables) by Antoine Dahdah, Libraire du Liban, Beirut, 1987. An Arabic-English edition has been published.

Safwat al-Bayan li Ma'ani al-Qur'an, Husayn M Makhluf, Kuwait, 1987.

Safwat at-Tafasir, (3 vols.) by Muhammad 'Ali as-Sabuni , Makkah, al-Mukarramah, 1980.

Translations of the Qur'an in English

The Message of the Qur'an by Muhammad Asad, Dar al-Andalus, Gibraltar, 1980

The Koran Interpreted, Arthur J Arberry, Oxford University Press, 1964

The Meaning of the Glorious Qur'an by Muhammad Marmaduke Pickthall, various editions available. A revised edition of this in 'modern standard English' by Arafat K El-Ashi has been published by Amana, Beltsville, USA, 1996

The Holy Qur'an - Text, translation and commentary by Abdullah Yusuf Ali, various editions available.

Tajwid (Qur'an recitation)

Tajwid al-Qur'an by Ashraf Abdul-Fattah, Aladdin Hassanin & Salah Saleh, Bakkah Publishing, London, 1989

Qur'an at-Tajwid, CDs, colour coded, repetition facility, (Mac & PC), Syria,

Qur'an Recordings

Muhammad Siddiq al-Minshawi, audiocassettes, CDs

Muhammad Khalil al-Husari, audiocassettes, CDs

Sudaysi, audiocassettes

General

Way to the Qur'an by Khurram Murad, Islamic Foundation, Leicester, 1986

Major Themes in the Qur'an by Fazlur Rahman, Bibliotheca Islamica, Chicago, 1980.

Qur'an in the Classroom by Adeleke Dirisu Ajijola, Islamic Publications, Lahore, 1977

'Ulum al-Qur'an by Ahmad von Denffer, Islamic Foundation, Leicester, 1983

MELS easy steps in Arabic

An attractive course in reading and writing the Arabic script
and reading the Qur'an. Well-graded and extensively tested, the course
makes learning the Arabic script **easy, quick and enjoyable**.
Now used by many schools and madrasahs throughout the world.
The course is suitable for self-study, for classroom use
or short, intensive courses.

THE COURSE COMPRISES

◆ **Alphabet Poster.**
Large (A2 size) and in colour. For letter recognition.
Attractive for classrooms and for homes.

◆ **Arabic Alphabet Song.**
A delightful song on cassette for children, and even for adults.
For use with the Alphabet Poster at home or in the classroom.

◆ **Arabic Flashcards.**
42 cards with all letters in their separate forms and some in joined forms.
Used to master letter recognition and for games.

◆ **Easy Steps in Qur'an Reading** (Pupil's Book).
64 pages. A carefully graded reader covering all the elements and rules
of reading.

◆ **Easy Steps in Qur'an Reading** (Teacher's/Self-study manual).
120 pages. Contains full explanatory notes in English for each page of
the Arabic text. Also, suggestions on how to use the course, and
teaching techniques.

◆ **Two audio cassettes** (running time: 60 min. each).
Contains the full text of ESQR. Each line of the text is identified to
make it easy to follow text and tape.

◆ **Easy Steps in Arabic Handwriting** (Workbooks 1 & 2).
32 pages each, A4 size. Well-graded. Begin with patterns to encourage
right to left movement. Special techniques to show how words are
built up from individual letters. Adequate space for tracing and
copying. Enjoyable exercises: word building, word search games. All
words used in the workbooks, except two, are from the Qur'an.

◆ **Arabic Alphabet Summary Chart.**
A4 size. A special and important feature of the course. Sets out
letters in their various forms. Introduces letters in words in a graded
sequence. Indispensable for ready reference and useful for quick
revision.

Available as a complete set or individual items. See Order Form.